Praying Girls Devotional

Praying Girls

Devotional

60 Days to **Shape Your Heart** and **Grow Your Faith** through **Prayer**

Sheila Walsh

BakerBooks

a division of Baker Publishing Group
Grand Rapids, Michigan

Published by Baker Books
a division of Baker Publishing Group
PO Box 6287, Grand Rapids, MI 49516-6287
www.bakerbooks.com

Printed in the United States of America

Library of Congress Cataloging-in-Publication Data
Names: Walsh, Sheila, 1956– author.
Title: Praying girls devotional : 60 days to shape your heart and grow your faith through prayer / Sheila Walsh.
Description: Grand Rapids, Michigan : Baker Books, a division of Baker Publishing Group, 2020. | Audience: Ages 11–14 | Audience: Grades 7–9
Identifiers: LCCN 2020008742 | ISBN 9781540900678 (cloth)
Subjects: LCSH: Girls—Prayers and devotions—Juvenile literature. | Girls—Religious life—Juvenile literature. | Christian life—Juvenile literature. | Devotional exercises—Juvenile literature.
Classification: LCC BV4860 .W356 2020 | DDC 242/.633—dc23
LC record available at https://lccn.loc.gov/2020008742

The author is represented by Dupree Miller and Associates, a global literary agency. www.dupreemiller.com

Interior design by William Overbeeke

20   21   22   23   24   25   26   7   6   5   4   3   2   1

This book is dedicated to every girl
who has ever longed to know
her heavenly Father better.
The wonderful news is that
you are seen,
you are known,
and you are loved.
God is listening.

For prayer is nothing else than being on
terms of friendship with God.

SAINT TERESA OF AVILA

Are You Coming?

A Note from Me to You

Sweet friend,

It's exciting to receive an invitation, isn't it? It might be an invitation to a friend's birthday party or to a school dance or to a competition in sports or debate. It feels good to have your presence requested, to know that someone *wants you to come.*

For more than two years, I've felt a strong call to prayer. I wake up nearly every morning *excited* to pray—and to ask others to pray with me. And so here is my invitation to you:

- Would you like to begin having a daily, ongoing conversation with God?
- Would you like to join me in seeing what God will do when His daughters decide to pray every day, believing He is with us?
- Will you join me on this adventure as we learn about the power of prayer?

If you're wanting to say yes to that invitation but are unsure about where to start, then this book is for you. In the pages to come, we will explore how to talk to God and why talking with God is the most important thing we can do for a happy and peace-filled life.

I wish I'd had a book like this when I was your age.

I wish someone had told me then what I understand now: God doesn't want your perfection; He just wants your presence.

God is on the move! And He wants us to be part of what He's up to. We can do just that through prayer. You are never alone. God is listening.

Your friend,

Sheila

Contents

A Peek at What's Inside

Hey, praying girl!
Here is a listing of the subjects for all sixty days.
Keep your favorite pen handy and check off each day as you go.

PART 1

When Life

Feels Hard

Have you ever noticed that just when things are
going great, something happens, or someone says
something, or doubt creeps into your thoughts that
makes it seem like everything is suddenly all wrong?

Life can be like that.

The good news? Despite how things seem, God says,
"I see you. I care about you. I'm here to help."

Is Anybody There?

You can be sure that I will be with you always.

MATTHEW 28:20 ERV

Everyone feels alone sometimes. Maybe you felt alone when you were sleeping over at a friend's house and started to miss your family more and more as the hours ticked by. Maybe you were sick and had to sit out an important event—a dance recital, your last soccer game of the season, an awards night—and as you sat there, all by yourself in your bedroom, you felt *really* alone. Or maybe you felt left out when you found out that some of your friends got together to hang out and you weren't invited. Later, they told you why you hadn't been invited, and the explanation made sense, but still, in the moment, you felt . . . *alone.*

Like I said, we all feel alone sometimes, but God tells us in the Bible that even when we *feel* alone, *we're never actually alone.*

During Jesus's final days here on earth, He met with His followers to tell them what they were supposed to do until He came back. Some of the people Jesus was talking to that day could hardly believe it was Him. He had been killed on a cross and buried in a tomb. And now He was back—in the flesh? He was. It *was* Jesus talking to them, and He had something very important to say. Here is the message He gave them according to Matthew 28:20:

You can be sure that I will be with you always. (ERV)

Jesus was telling His followers—and us too!—that if there is one thing we can be sure of, it's that He is with us every day. In fact, if you have given your heart to Jesus, then you will never live a single minute of your life without Him right there by your side.

Pause and Pray

God, thank You for promising that I'll never be alone in this world and that You will be with me all day today—right there in the middle of every situation, every conversation, and every challenge I face. It feels so good to know that You are near to me and that You love me. I love You too. Amen.

Reflect and Write

Based on this prayer, what can you choose to tell yourself the next time you feel alone?

....

....

....

What If I Stink at This?

> Meanwhile, the moment we get tired in the waiting,
> God's Spirit is right alongside helping us along. If we
> don't know how or what to pray, it doesn't matter.
> He does our praying in and for us, making prayer
> out of our wordless sighs, our aching groans.
>
> ROMANS 8:26 MESSAGE

Praying to God can feel funny. For starters, He's invisible. How do you talk to someone you can't see? When I was a kid, I remember being totally confused about this prayer thing. I was so intimidated to talk to the Creator of the universe. I was just sure that if I said the wrong thing, I'd either embarrass myself or make Him mad! Once I got over that fear and started praying, prayer *still* felt hard for me. I'd get bored. Or distracted. Or run out of things to say. After one of those uninspired "prayer sessions," I muttered, "I think I stink at this."

Have you ever felt like you stink at prayer? You may *never* run out of things to say to your closest friends, but when you try to say one complete sentence to God, you totally freeze up. It's frustrating, isn't it?

I want to share a verse with you that may help you the next time you try to pray. In Romans 8:26, the apostle Paul reminds us of an amazing truth:

> Meanwhile, the moment we get tired in the waiting, God's Spirit is right alongside helping us along. If we don't know how or what to pray, it doesn't matter. He does our praying in and for us, making prayer out of our wordless sighs, our aching groans. (Message)

The beauty of this verse is that when you need God's help but have no clue what to say, you can take a deep breath and *tell Him that*. Literally. You can close your eyes and say, "God, I don't know what to say." This verse in Romans assures us that God's Spirit will take things from there. As you sit quietly, thinking about God, opening your hands to all that God has for you, longing for things like peace and patience and kindness to take root in you, God the Holy Spirit will whisper what you need to God the Father.

Give it a try. If you don't know how to tell God about the burdens that are weighing you down today, let His Spirit do the talking. You might sit on your bed with your palms turned upward ready to receive from God. Close your eyes and exhale all of your concerns. Then whisper God's name aloud. Tell Him you're not sure what to say. Ask Him to help you sort out your thoughts and feelings. Be honest. Be real. You don't stink at prayer!

Pause and Pray

God, help me to remember today that it doesn't really matter what I say to You or how I say it. What matters is that I come to You in prayer, intentionally inviting You into my day and into my life, trusting You to help me be the kind of person You created me to be. Amen.

Reflect and Write

How does it make you feel to know that you don't have to say the "right things" to God in prayer?

....

....

....

Who Am I?

You are not what the world makes you;
but you are children of God.

HENRI NOUWEN

If I were to ask, "Who are you?" how would you answer? Maybe you'd tell me your name. "I'm Sophie." "I'm Emma." "I'm Madison."

You might tell me your grade or the name of your school. "I'm in sixth grade at Columbus Middle School." "I'm a fourth grader at Hopkins Elementary." "I'm homeschooled."

You might tell me a few details that explain why we're crossing paths. If we met in a library, for instance, you might tell me what you're studying. Or if we met in an airport, you might tell me where you and your family are headed.

You might tell me a few things you're interested in. "I'm a dancer." "I'm on the swim team." "I love to ride horses." "I've played soccer since I could walk."

When we think of who we are, we tend to think in terms of the name we go by, the groups we're a part of, where we are in this big, beautiful world, or the way we spend our time.

It's true that those things are important and that they make up a big part of who we are. But did you know that if you are a follower of Jesus, there is something about you that is more important than any of those things? It has to do not just with who you are but with *Whose* you are. You can read about it for yourself in 1 John 3:1:

> The Father has loved us so much! This shows how much he loved us: We are called children of God. And we really are his children. (ERV)

If Christ is in you, then you are a child of God, a daughter of the one, true King. You might change your name if you get married. You might start going to a different school. Your circumstances might change ten thousand times. But this one thing will always be true: *you are a child of God.*

Pause and Pray

God, when I think about who I am, I want to think first about being Your child. Thank You for creating me. Thank You for loving me. Thank You for accepting me. Thank You for adopting me into Your forever family. Whatever else happens today, it's so good to know that with You I am always at home. Amen.

Reflect and Write

What encouragement can you take from the reminder that at the core of who you are, you are a daughter of the King? What do you think would change about the way you engage with other people if you were absolutely, 100 percent sure that you are a beloved member of God's forever family and that He is thrilled to have you for a daughter?

....

....

....

Help!

Prayer will change a heartache into a cheerful song.

ELDRED HERBERT

When was the last time you got yourself into a sticky situation and really, really needed help to get out of it? If you've ever tried to carry too many things upstairs at once, or waited until the last minute to study for a test, or accidentally locked yourself out of the house, or broken a treasured vase that belonged to your grandmother, then you know exactly what I'm talking about. Sometimes we desperately need help. And we need it *now*.

The book of Psalms, which is in the Old Testament, was originally a songbook for the Jewish people. Each psalm was a song they would sing to God, and many times the verses and choruses would give them strength when things felt hard. Psalm 46:1, for example, says this:

> God is our refuge and strength,
> always ready to help in times of trouble.

Long ago, the people singing this song needed God's help to find food during a famine or to be healed from some awful disease or to escape their enemies, who were trying to enslave and even kill them. These days you might sing the song for completely different reasons. Maybe things have gotten sideways between you and a close friend. Maybe you've been having horrible headaches lately and can't figure out why. Maybe your confidence has been sinking, and you're not sure how to pull it back up.

Maybe math class is a nightmare.

Maybe your dad just lost his job.

Maybe your friend told someone your secret.

Maybe you don't agree with your parents' decision not to let you have a phone.

Whatever is bugging you today, you can sing this debugging song: "God is my refuge and strength, always ready to help in times of trouble."

God is near! He is able! He longs to help you in times of need.

Pause and Pray

God, it is definitely good news that You are available to help me whenever I find myself needing help. Thank You for taking my needs seriously and for restoring my hope. Amen.

Reflect and Write

What situation is bugging you most today? What might God's help look like for you?

....

....

....

Why Is Life So Confusing?

Trust GOD from the bottom of your heart;
 don't try to figure out everything on your own.
Listen for GOD's voice in everything
 you do, everywhere you go;
 he's the one who will keep you on track.

PROVERBS 3:5–6 MESSAGE

If you're like most people your age, you were a little bit (or a lot!) confused when you first learned how to do double-digit multiplication. Multiplying one digit by one digit is one thing, but somehow adding numbers to that tens column makes people wonder if their heads might explode.

So many numbers!

So many columns!

So many operations to execute!

If only we could return to the days of 2+2=4, right? Things were far less confusing then.

Worse than being faced with a confusing math problem is being faced with a confusing *life* problem. For instance, what are you supposed to do when a trusted friend confides in you by telling you a secret, but keeping that secret might mean standing by while your friend gets into trouble? *Confusing*.

Or what about when your parents restrict your screen time, even as your big brother or sister seems to be on his or her phone 24/7? *Confusing*.

How about when you ask a teacher for help and are told you have to "figure it out on your own." *Confusing*.

It's true. The world can be a confusing place. Which is why it's such good news that there is one place we can go where we'll *never* be confused. That place is in the presence of God.

In Proverbs 3:5–6, we read:

> Trust GOD from the bottom of your heart;
>   don't try to figure out everything on your own.
> Listen for GOD's voice in everything you do, everywhere
>   you go;
>   he's the one who will keep you on track. (Message)

That's quite a promise, don't you think? Whenever we take a step toward God, we simultaneously take a step away from confusion and disorder. Why? Because God is a God of order. Of harmony.

If you've ever been to the symphony, then you know that things sound pretty awful when everyone is warming up, playing his or her own music. The word for this is *cacophony*, and it's tough on the ears. But once the conductor puts the baton up in the air and leads the group through the first few notes, the sound that comes from those various instruments is beautiful. Why? In a word: *harmony*. Everyone is playing the right notes at the right time and in concert with the other musicians.

Likewise, when those of us who love God lay down our own music for the sake of playing the notes that God has asked us to play, the sounds that come from our lives are pitch-perfect and sweet. When we look to Him for wisdom and understanding, we find a path that leads us to peace.

Pause and Pray

God, I am so grateful that You bring a sense of order and peace to things that completely confuse me. Help me to remember to come to You whenever I'm feeling confused, trusting that You will show me how to make sense of things. Amen.

Reflect and Write

What situation or relationship seems most confusing to you these days and why? What help do you wish God would provide?

....

....

....

Just Blah

Today me will live in the moment unless it's
unpleasant, in which case me will eat a cookie.

COOKIE MONSTER

Not every day will be a best day kind of day. You've probably learned that by now. Some days will be long. Some days will be average. Some days will be just . . . *blah.*
You have to get out of your comfy bed way too early.
School drags on forever.
You have to miss practice because your knee is still hurting.
Your mom makes chicken for dinner . . . again.
Your assigned reading is duller than dull.
Blah. Blah. Blah.
Some days are just plain *blah.*
But even when a day starts that way, it doesn't have to *stay* that way. Why? Because God loves to better our blahs.
In Psalm 119, we read of a man who was having a very blah day. He was sad and lonely and feeling sorry for himself when a thought occurred to him . . . a thought that just might help. He said to God:

> I weep with sorrow;
>   encourage me by your word. . . .
> I will pursue your commands,
>   for you expand my understanding. (vv. 28, 32)

Now, you may not be "weeping with sorrow," as the psalmist was, but is there some part of you that can relate? Do you need a fresh dose of energy? Do you long for encouragement to come your way? If so, then reach for your Bible and look up the verses below. How might these words better *your* blahs today?

- 2 Corinthians 12:9–10
- Psalm 31:24
- John 16:33

Pause and Pray

God, on days when things feel kind of blah, I love remembering that You still see me, that You still love me, and that You're still working in my life. Help me to rest in that knowledge. Help me to be just as content with the quiet sameness of life as I am with the exciting events. Amen.

Reflect and Write

Why do you think it's important to learn how to deal with blah days when they come along?

....

....

....

Never Enough

So since we find ourselves fashioned into all these
excellently formed and marvelously functioning
parts in Christ's body, let's just go ahead and
be what we were made to be, without enviously
or pridefully comparing ourselves with each
other, or trying to be something we aren't.

ROMANS 12:6 MESSAGE

I'm going to tell you a secret. There's a trap that's easy to fall into. It's called the comparison trap.

You're not the only one who struggles with comparing yourself to others and coming out on the losing end. I've done it too. Everyone I know struggles at times with comparison. Even the smartest, prettiest, most talented people alive compare themselves to the people they think are smarter, prettier, and more talented than they are. Nobody escapes the comparison trap. At some point, we all fall in.

That's the bad news.

The good news is this: we can hop right out of that trap and move on with our day.

Let me show you how.

Let's say you're really into ballet. You've been training for six years straight and are feeling pretty good about your skill level these days. You can nail a double pirouette, and you can execute a perfect *saut de chat* leap. But then *she* moves to town and joins your dance class. She is your same age. Your same level. Has danced the same number of years as you. And yet, she is somehow . . . *better.*

Much, much better.

She looks like she was born wearing pointe shoes. She never misses a turn. She never gets winded. She never looks confused. Ugh. You thought you were doing well in ballet until *that* girl came along.

You've fallen into the comparison trap. Now, what should you do?

I'd like to pause for a moment and read a verse of Scripture with you. It's from Romans 12:6:

> Let's just go ahead and be what we were made to be, without envi-ously or pridefully comparing ourselves with each other, or trying to be something we aren't. (Message)

The verse tells us to go ahead and be who we were made to be. Don't try to be something or someone that you are not.

Back to our ballet scenario. If you were to go to class thinking not about how crummy you feel around that new dancer but rather about how to look and act like Jesus in her presence, what do you suppose might change?

Maybe instead of being jealous of that new girl, you would welcome her graciously to class.

Maybe instead of giving her the cold shoulder, you would let compassion lead the way.

Maybe instead of working to look better than her, you would encourage her in her dancing.

The point is this: rather than focusing our attention on compar-ing ourselves to others, we can focus our attention on becoming more like God. And when that is how we choose to spend our days, we will be *exactly* who God made us to be.

Pause and Pray

God, it is so hard sometimes to feel like I'm enough! There are so many people who are smarter than I am, prettier than I am, more capable than I am, more loving than I am, more . . . everything . . . than I am—or at least that's how it feels. I hate feeling less than. I hate feeling insecure. And yet every day it seems like I fall into those traps. I'm ready to steer clear of them! Please help me to remember that You have made me on purpose for a purpose and that the only person I need to be is me. You have a plan for me, and I want to use every bit of my energy to pursue that plan alone. Amen.

Reflect and Write

What special plan for your life do you think you might miss if you spend all your time and energy being envious of someone else?

....

....

....

Why Did I Do That?

Guilt tells us that we've done something wrong.
Shame tells us that we are something wrong.

SHEILA WALSH

Sometimes the tears come as a flood.

We made a mistake, and we were caught in our mistake, and now we're being asked to talk about the mistake we made. And it feels like agony having to explain how we messed up and having to hear about how wrong we were when we already know we were wrong. We *know* we were wrong. Do we really have to relive the whole thing?

We choke up before the words even come. And then come the tears—filling our eyes, clouding our vision, streaming down our cheeks. It feels so bad to be in the wrong, so very, very bad.

And yet we're the ones who tend to make things far worse.

An interesting passage in the Bible explains what we should do about our mistakes. First John 1:8–9 says this:

If we claim we have no sin, we are only fooling ourselves and not living in the truth. But if we confess our sins to him, he is faithful and just to forgive us our sins and to cleanse us from all wickedness.

The first verse in the passage reminds us that we are, in fact, going to make mistakes. The truth is that we *will* goof up, we *will* make mistakes, we *will* sin. The second verse reminds us that we don't have to stay stuck in a cycle of sadness and sorrow. What's more, we don't have to feel ashamed.

Whew!

Let me say that last part again. We don't have to feel ashamed. You never have to experience shame.

What can you do instead? Confess your mistake to God. Tell Him you're sorry for goofing up. Claim the forgiveness He says is yours. Ask Him to make you perfectly clean. And then watch as that flood of grief and shame is beautifully, miraculously dried up.

Pause and Pray

God, thank You for showing me that there is a big difference between hating the mistakes I make and hating myself for making them. Help me to love myself as You love me, even when I goof up. Help me to trust You to forgive me for my sins and to make all things new once more. Amen.

Reflect and Write

Why do you think it's so hard to forgive yourself for the mistakes you make? Why do you suppose God longs for you to forgive yourself as He promises to forgive you?

....

....

....

Feeling Blue

I prayed to the LORD, and he answered me.
He freed me from all my fears.

PSALM 34:4

There's a saying people use when they're having not just a bad day or two but a whole string of not-great days. "Feeling blue"—that's what they say, as in, "I've been feeling a little blue . . ."

"Feeling blue" means feeling weary and anxious and sad. It means you don't have your usual energy. You don't have your usual spark. You don't have your usual creativity. You don't have your usual flair. You're not as chatty when you're blue. You're not as hopeful either. You're not as imaginative or optimistic or glad. Feeling blue means you're feeling less than yourself, as though someone has turned the bright light inside of you down to the dimmest of dim.

Some girls have felt blue because someone they loved was struggling with chronic illness or pain.

Some girls have felt blue because they were being bullied at school.

Some girls have felt blue because they felt like they didn't have a close friend.

Some girls have felt blue because they lost someone precious to them.

I've felt blue before. When I was a full-grown adult, long after I'd decided to follow Jesus at age eleven, I felt the bluest I'd ever felt. I was so blue that I had to go to a hospital where they specialized in treating the blues. The first night I was there I lay on the floor of my hospital room, begging God to remove my despair. And do you know what He did for me? He reminded me that I didn't have to stay blue.

I want to show you the passage of Scripture He led me to that night. It's Psalm 34:4–6. If you are feeling blue, then these verses are just for you.

> I prayed to the LORD, and he answered me.
>   He freed me from all my fears.
> Those who look to him for help will be radiant with joy;
>   no shadow of shame will darken their faces.
> In my desperation I prayed, and the LORD listened;
>   he saved me from all my troubles.

You can be freed from all your fears.

You can be radiant with joy.

You can be spared the shadow of shame.

You can be saved from the trouble you're in or the trouble that feels as if it's in you.

And how are these things accomplished for you? By *praying*—praying to the Lord—and by waiting patiently for His reply.

Pause and Pray

God, thank You for hearing my prayers when I'm having a good day, and thank You for hearing my prayers when I'm feeling blue. I want the things the Bible talks about—fearlessness and radiance and joy. Will You give me these gifts today, Father? Will You show me how to trust You for them? Amen.

Reflect and Write

When have you or someone you love felt blue? What is the hardest part about feeling blue?

....

....

....

Ghosted by God

God is the friend of silence.

_____

MOTHER TERESA

Have you ever thought someone was listening to you only to realize that they weren't paying attention to you at all? You sat there, pouring out your heart to your friend, explaining some struggle you were in and how it was making you feel, and then you looked up to find that she was texting someone on her phone! Devastating, right? We all deeply long to feel heard, and when a friend isn't doing her part to listen to us, it can feel like a slap in the face.

Worse still is when we don't feel heard by God.

You may have heard of a man in the Bible named Job. Job loved God and was faithful to follow God every day. And yet Job faced real suffering in life. _Everything_, it seemed, had gone wrong. Job went from being the richest man on earth to losing all of it in the blink of an eye. Most devastating of all, he lost all his children. Yet the one thing he never lost through it all was his steadfast faith in God.

To put this in modern terms, it would be like losing all your siblings, all your friends, all your clothes, all your pets, all your devices, everything. _Shocking_, right? What on earth would you do?

This is the predicament in which Job found himself, and yet he still trusted in God.

I bring up the story of Job because there will probably come a time in your life when you feel a little bit ghosted by God. You will stumble into a struggle one day, and despite your fervent prayers toward heaven, you just won't sense a reply. "God?" you'll ask the ceiling and walls. "God? Are you still there?"

I want to remind you that in that moment, even if there is no reply, even if there is nothing but silence surrounding you, the answer is yes.

Yes! God is still near to you.

Yes! God still cares.

Yes! God still sees you.

Yes! God's love is real.

So what do you do when you can't *feel* that love? What do you do when you don't *sense* that God is near? Let's look at the story of Job to find out how Job navigated that path. In response to all those losses and to God's seeming silence as well, Job said this in Job 1:21:

> I came naked from my mother's womb
>> and I will be naked when I leave.
> The LORD gave me what I had,
>> and the LORD has taken it away.
> Praise the name of the LORD!

Job didn't get to that place overnight. He was angry, confused, and hurt, but he brought all those feelings to God and was able to come to a place of peace.

Interestingly, by God's grace, we can do the same. We can live like Job every day. We get to tell God the whole truth.

During those seasons when we struggle to hear God's voice, we can spend our time refreshing our faith, reminding ourselves that every good blessing we have is from God and that His name is forever to be praised.

Pause and Pray

God, You are good, and You are holy. You are above all else!
And even when I don't hear Your still, small whisper, I choose
to praise Your name. Amen.

Reflect and Write

Why do you think God seems quiet from time to time? What might
He be inviting you to learn during those seasons?

. . . .

. . . .

. . . .

Will I Ever Be Cool?

Don't be selfish; don't try to impress others.
Be humble, thinking of others as better than
yourselves. Don't look out only for your own
interests, but take an interest in others, too.

PHILIPPIANS 2:3–4

Let's say your history teacher gives you an assignment to write a paper on the American Revolution. He gives you all the specifics for the paper—how many pages it needs to be, how many sources you need to cite, the date the paper is due, and so forth. You dutifully pull out your planner and write down the assignment so that you don't forget to do it. But instead of logging the subject of the paper as "the American Revolution," you write down "the French Revolution."

That weekend you head to the library to start doing research for your paper. You check out the right number of books and feverishly write the right number of pages. On the right day, you turn in your paper. But to your utter horror, you get that paper back two days later and see that you've earned a failing grade.

"But I worked so hard!" you explain to your teacher. "I used the right number of sources and wrote the right number of pages and turned in the paper on *exactly* the right day!" To which your teacher says, "Yes, but you did the *wrong assignment*, which means all that effort was in vain." You thought you were supposed to be giving everything you had to one thing, but it was the wrong thing. What if that's true of finding out who God wants you to be as well?

If you are like every girl who has gone before you, then you want to be cool, you want to fit in. You want to have the right clothes and the right hairstyle and the right devices. You want to go to the right places and be with the right crowd. And there's nothing inherently wrong with those desires. It's just that they shouldn't take priority in our lives.

In Philippians 2:3–4, the apostle Paul says these words:

> Don't be selfish; don't try to impress others. Be humble, thinking of others as better than yourselves. Don't look out only for your own interests, but take an interest in others, too.

We can spend an entire lifetime trying to be cool, but at the end of it all, we will face the same reaction from God that your history teacher had. "Yes, I see that you were passionate about fitting in," He'll say, "but that's not the assignment I gave you. The assignment was to be humble. To serve others. To stop trying so hard to impress . . ."

In another place in Scripture, God promises to promote people who surrender their lives fully to Him. Which ought to come as good news to us! We don't have to promote ourselves. God will take care of that when we decide to trust Him.

Pause and Pray

God, I admit that I can get pretty wrapped up in looking and acting a certain way so that I fit in with people I think are cool. And yet I think what You're saying is that the coolest of all is a girl who is humble and kind. Please show me how to humble myself and how to consider others' needs instead of only my own. Amen.

Reflect and Write

What could you do to take an interest in others today?

....

....

....

I Blew It!

Grace is love stooping.

―――――――

ELIZABETH WALSH

Remembering that we are saved not by the things we do (or don't do) but by God's perfect gift of grace is probably the hardest part of the Christian life. This is especially hard to remember when we've done something we shouldn't do or neglected to do something we should. For example, have you ever done the following things?

- told a lie to get out of trouble
- saw a friend in need and were too busy to help
- blamed someone else for something you did wrong
- done something your parents asked you not to do

When we do these things, we feel terrible inside just waiting to get caught. And the tendency as we sink under the weight of that sin is to think that God loves us less.

I spent my entire childhood and most of my young-adult years trying to perform for God. I believed that if I did all the right things, prayed all the right prayers, avoided all the "really bad" sins, and generally followed the rules, then He would be super-pleased with me and life would go well for me.

Boy, did I have that wrong.

I could have saved myself a lot of effort if I'd realized that God was pleased with me from the start! What God wanted wasn't my *performance*; what He wanted was my *heart*.

If God's acceptance of us were based on something we could control, then we would think *we* were the reason we were saved. No, God accomplishes salvation through *grace*, which is receiving what we don't deserve so that all glory belongs to *Him*. Look at what Ephesians 2:8–10 says:

> Saving is all his [God's] idea, and all his work. All we do is trust him enough to let him do it. It's God's gift from start to finish! We don't play the major role. If we did, we'd probably go around bragging that we'd done the whole thing! No, we neither make nor save ourselves. God does both the making and saving. He creates each of us by Christ Jesus to join him in the work he does, the good work he has gotten ready for us to do, work we had better be doing. (Message)

Because God is the One who saves us, and because we are saved by His grace and not by our works, nothing we do can make Him love us more or less. His love is the same no matter what.

You don't have to perform to win God's acceptance or love. All you must do is hand Him your heart.

Pause and Pray

God, what a relief it is to know that even when I blow it, I can't blow up Your love for me. Thank You for the gift of grace. I accept that great gift today. Amen.

Reflect and Write

How would your feelings about your self-worth change right now if you fully accepted God's grace?

....

....

....

Broken

It's a beautiful thing that God will do with a broken heart if you give Him all the pieces.

SHEILA WALSH

Is there a part of you that feels broken . . . unfixable . . . not quite right?

When I was about your age, I hated my bad skin and greasy hair. They drove me nuts! No matter what I tried, I was stuck with a broken look. I remember seeing other girls with their long, healthy hair and perfectly clear skin and thinking, *If only I could look like that . . .*

It was agony to feel broken.

It was miserable to feel not right.

I know girls who feel broken because they stink at sports. They try out for everything they can try out for and yet never make the team.

I know girls who feel broken because others see them as bossy. They work so hard to be cooperative and inclusive and yet still wind up telling everyone what to do.

I know girls who feel broken because they are shy. They have plenty of thoughts and ideas in their heads but are reluctant to speak their minds.

On and on we could go, making a list of all the brokenness we could find. My broken places. Your broken places. The seemingly unfixable things we all share. And yet to *all* those broken things, God's response is the same: "I will heal them. I will redeem them. I will fix them and use them for good."

Here is how the psalmist said it in Psalm 147:3:

> He [God] heals the brokenhearted
> and bandages their wounds.

God promises to take whatever broken things we give Him and bring beauty from them somehow. Like a surgeon who sets a broken bone and wraps a cast around it until it heals, God sets things right from the inside out, asking us to trust Him each step of the way.

So for now, bring Him your broken things with confidence. Ask Him to heal you from the inside out. Trust that His transformative work will have its way in your life. Let the grand fixing officially begin.

Pause and Pray

God, I hate the parts of me that feel broken. More than anything, I want them fixed. And yet I know that Scripture says that You actually use broken things for good. What good do You have in store for me, Father, good that will come to me through this broken thing? I pray for patience to wait on Your goodness to me. I pray for Your will to be done in my life. Amen.

Reflect and Write

A health scare can bring a family closer together. A natural disaster can cause people to feel more grateful for what they have. The loss of a job can prompt a husband and wife to be more present with each other. Saying good-bye to a beloved teacher can make room for an even better teacher to emerge. When have you seen something good come from brokenness in your own life or in the life of someone you love?

....

....

....

Ouch

> Giving thanks is that: making the canyon of pain into a
> megaphone to proclaim the ultimate goodness of God
> when Satan and all the world would sneer at us to recant.
>
> ANN VOSKAMP

If you've ever had a hope that just didn't pan out, then you know the pain I'm talking about here. You wanted the lead in the school musical, but it went to someone else. You reached out to befriend a new classmate, but she didn't really want to be friends. You searched and searched for a missing beloved object, but it never showed up.

Or what about pain of a deeper sort? Maybe you're an only child who so wants a sibling. Or you're a peacemaker who wishes your parents could get along. Maybe you adore books but wrestle with dyslexia. Maybe your mind is healthy but your body is diseased.

There is pain, and then there is *pain*—but all pain makes us hurt.

Many years ago, I changed the way I prayed to God. I didn't change what I said. I just started saying it as though Jesus were in the room. I was in a lot of emotional pain at the time, and it seemed like too much to bear. I felt desperate and longed for relief. I believed Jesus could help.

I sat down in a chair and pulled up a chair in front of mine— you know, where Jesus could sit. I looked at that empty chair and envisioned Jesus there, eyes tender and arms opened wide. "Tell me everything," I pictured Him saying. "Tell me about every pain you feel . . ."

And so I did just that.

It felt so good to get every last thing off my chest that night, to have someone listen to all my pain. The funny thing was that the more I talked, the lighter my burden felt, as if Jesus was literally taking it from me. It was like I was living—in person—the promise of Matthew 11:28:

> Come to me, all of you who are weary and carry heavy burdens, and I will give you rest.

Two verses later, Jesus promises His followers that His yoke is easy to bear and His burden is light. Isn't that a great exchange?

Pretend for a moment that you don't like Brussels sprouts and that you really, really like chocolate cake. Imagine someone coming up to you and saying, "Hey, I see that you have three pounds of Brussels sprouts on your dinner plate. If you give me those, I'll give you this massive, sixteen-layer chocolate cake."

Done and done, right?

This is like Jesus's exchange. "You give me your heavy burden," He says, "and I'll give you one that is light."

Who wouldn't want *that* trade, I ask you?

Nobody—that's who.

And so a challenge. If you're in pain, have a seat. Pull up an empty chair. Tell Jesus about every last thing that hurts. Take His light burden in exchange for your weighty one.

Pause and Pray

God, it is wonderful to realize that while the pain I some-times feel is real, Your willingness to bear it is even more real. Thank you. Thank You for grace, which helps me to hand You my pain, and for peace, which shows up in pain's place. I love You, Father. I trust You with my pain today. Amen.

Reflect and Write

What pain can you hand to Jesus today? What burden will you allow Him to bear?

....

....

....

Unworthy

I know that God has a plan, and He
is doing something new.

SHEILA WALSH

When I was a young adult, I went through a few months when life felt altogether overwhelming. I had decided to go to seminary (Bible school) because I thought God wanted me to be a missionary. But by the time I got there, I had lost confidence that this was what God really wanted. I was confused and frustrated and worried that I was in the wrong place. To make matters worse, everyone else seemed to know exactly what they were supposed to be doing. It was scary, to say the least.

As my graduation day drew near, I begged God more and more to show me what to do. "What am I supposed to do?" I'd ask Him through tears. "Where am I supposed to go? How am I supposed to serve You?"

I wanted to serve God more than anything else in my whole life, and yet I had no idea what that meant. When answers didn't come quickly enough, I feared He didn't want my service at all. Maybe I wasn't worthy enough to serve Him. Maybe God wanted someone else to do my job. The other students *did* look worthier than I felt. Maybe I wasn't cut out for this.

I felt damaged.

I felt broken.

I felt unworthy.

I felt sad.

I kept looking back over my life and at all the fears and insecurities I had. Each day I would cry and pray and cry and pray some more. Finally, during one of those prayer times, I read the words of Isaiah 43:18–19:

> Forget about what's happened;
>> don't keep going over old history.
> Be alert, be present. I'm about to do something
>> brand-new.
>> It's bursting out! Don't you see it?
> There it is! I'm making a road through the desert,
>> rivers in the badlands. (Message)

You know what? Those verses were right! God *was* doing a new thing in my life. I just needed to trust Him so that I could walk in it.

Which brings me to this truth: He is doing a new thing in your life too. Don't you see it? There it is! He is carving a new path for you. He is making a new way for you. He is putting together a new opportunity for you. He is bringing water to the deserts of your life.

He is doing these things for you.

You, who are worthy.

You, who are *His*.

Choose to see the new thing today.

Pause and Pray

God, sometimes I think You're eager to bless other people but not me. I imagine that You're looking for people who are better than I am, who are more disciplined than I am, who are kinder than I am, who don't forget to finish their homework or take out the trash like I sometimes do. I do wonder . . . wouldn't You rather bless people like that?

Thank You for the reminder that You find me worthy too. Thank You that You are doing something new in my life, something that will bless me, that will bring gladness to my heart and life. Amen.

Reflect and Write

What new thing do you hope God is up to in your life?

....

....

....

PART 2

Not My

Best Self

When we think everything is going wrong, we
act in ways that are wrong too.

We pout.
We get angry.
We lose hope.
We quit believing God.

Thankfully, God does not quit believing in us.
"My grace is sufficient for you," He promises.
He promises to walk with us each day.

Freaking Out

Temper, temper!

SCAR TO MUFASA IN *THE LION KING*

We've all been there. The stresses of life, the pressure we put on ourselves to be perfect, the comparisons we make to everyone around us . . . at some point, it's all just too much. The only solution we see? Freaking. Out.

Did you ever see the cartoon *Peg Plus Cat*? In each episode, a little girl named Peg and her sidekick encounter a new problem to solve, one that happens to require some pretty sophisticated math skills. Inevitably, the problem makes her feel like her head is going to explode. In response, she shouts, "I'm totally freaking out!"

Life has that effect sometimes, doesn't it? Even if we don't say it out loud, on the *inside*, we feel just like Peg. We're totally freaking out!

We think there is no other option than to freak out, but did you know that freaking out is always a *choice* we make? That's right. Letting our thoughts spin out of control and our emotions reach fever pitch and our hands tremble with frustration and fear is something we do to ourselves.

I know it doesn't seem this way. It seems like outside forces are *making* us freak out. But God's Word says that is not the case. Look at this promise Jesus made just before He left his earthly ministry and returned to heaven, to His Father's side:

I'm leaving you well and whole. That's my parting gift to you. Peace. I don't leave you the way you're used to being left—feeling abandoned, bereft. So don't be upset. Don't be distraught. (John 14:27 Message)

When Jesus departed earth, He left us with a gift. That gift was *peace*. And the best part was this: He put that gift *inside of us* in the form of His Holy Spirit so that whenever we need to open it, it is right there ready for us.

So the next time you think there is no other option than to totally freak out, give peace a try. Ask God to help you make the choice for peace. Pull out the gift God graciously gave you, and let it have its way.

Pause and Pray

God, I guess I never really thought about the fact that I have a choice to make when I feel like I'm going to freak out. And if freaking out is a choice, then I can choose something different instead. Today, Father, I want to choose peace. When life feels too heavy for me, please remind me that I can choose peace. I can exhale my frustration. I can take a deep breath. I can look to You for strength and stability. And I can let peace have its peaceful way. Amen.

Reflect and Write

When was the last time you freaked out? What did your freak-out experience involve? What happened as a result? What do you think about the experience, looking back on it now? What might have been different about your response if you had chosen peace instead?

....

....

....

Hide and Seek

I don't really understand myself, for I want
to do what is right, but I don't do it.

ROMANS 7:15

Have you ever eaten something that you knew wasn't good for you? I have. I love, love, love Ben & Jerry's ice cream, even though it doesn't love me back when I eat way too much of it. I know people who are allergic to dairy or to gluten or to blue food coloring, and yet from time to time, they just *have to have* some cheese, or some bread, or a cupcake covered with sky-colored sprinkles. And so they go for it, eating the very thing that will make them feel terrible later on.

I've noticed that we tend to behave this way with God, doing the opposite of what will help us succeed. When we have done something wrong or when we're hurting inside or when life seems like it's too much to bear, it's all too easy to run away from God, to hide from God, to try to clean up our mess on our own. This is not a good strategy for life, even when it seems like the best thing to do.

A far better approach is this one, which shows up in James 4:8:

Come close to God, and God will come close to you.

When we are hurting, or embarrassed, or frustrated, or in pain, the best thing we can do is not to hide from God but rather to run toward Him and hide ourselves there. Why? Because whenever we come close to our heavenly Father, as the verse says, He then comes close to us. And guess what else comes close to us whenever God the Father is near?

Divine strength.

Divine power.

Divine wisdom.

Divine grace.

Divine forgiveness.

Divine healing.

Divine insight.

Divine love.

Whatever you're in need of today, God possesses. And as you choose to hide yourself in Him—by praying to Him, by reading His Word, by doing His will, and by following His ways instead of coming up with your own plan—He will give those things to you.

Pause and Pray

God, I don't want to hide from You anymore. I want to come close to You, even in my pain, and trust that You will come close to me. Amen.

Reflect and Write

How will you come close to God today?

....

....

....

Way Too Many Worries

Don't fret or worry. Instead of worrying, pray.

PHILIPPIANS 4:6 MESSAGE

I have an experiment for you to try. Think of three things you're worried about today. Maybe you have a big test at school this week or a big dance performance in a few days that you're nervous about. Maybe you've been suffering with a head cold and are just sure you'll never feel better again. Perhaps you and a close friend have been struggling to get along, and it feels like your heart might break. Maybe you're worried about something else entirely. Whatever your worries are, I want you to hold them in your mind for a minute.

Got them? Three of them in mind? Write them down in the space below.

My biggest worries today are . . .

1. ....

2. ....

3. ....

Next I want you to think of three things you love most about God. Maybe you love the fact that He accepts you just as you are. Or maybe you love His grace, this idea that you don't have to earn your way with God, that because of Jesus He offers you salvation as a gift. Maybe what you love most about God is His forgiveness. No matter what you do, you can be completely forgiven and beautifully restored into relationship with Him—boom, just like that.

Do you have your three things? Go ahead and write them below. My favorite things about God are . . .

1. ....

2. ....

3. ....

Now here is the experiment. I want you to read aloud your list of worries several times in a row *while at the same time* thinking about the things you love about God. As your voice speaks the things you are worried about, I want your mind to stay focused on God. Ready to give it a try? On your mark, get set, go.

How did you do?

Philippians 4:8 says this:

And now, dear brothers and sisters, one final thing. Fix your thoughts on what is true, and honorable, and right, and pure, and lovely, and admirable. Think about things that are excellent and worthy of praise.

Why do you think the apostle Paul tells us to think about things that are good and honorable and excellent? Because, as you probably just noticed, it's impossible to talk about bad things when you're focused on what is good. You can choose to do one or the other, but you can't do both at the same time.

So go ahead and make a list of worries as often as you need to in order to get those pesky things off your mind. But then turn your attention to excellent things, such as those things you adore about God. As you think of His goodness and mercy, His provision and acceptance and peace, your worries will start to fade into the background, where you won't notice them at all.

Pause and Pray

God, I've never really stopped to think about the fact that I can hold only one type of thought in my mind at a time, but given this reality, I want to choose to think about You. Amen.

Reflect and Write

What will you tell yourself to do the next time you're overwhelmed by worry and fear?

....

....

....

Hello, Hope?

Just when you think the night will
never end, morning comes.

SHEILA WALSH

Her name was Hannah, spelled the same both forward and back, and her deepest hope in life was to be a mom. She was at the age when all of her friends had already had children, and yet there she was, not even one child to call her own.

She begged God to let her be a mother, telling Him she would raise this child to worship God. But still no son, no daughter, no tiny feet scampering across the floor.

Now, before I tell you what happened to Hannah, I want to ask you a question: Have you ever hoped for something as deeply as Hannah hoped for a child? Have you ever wanted something that urgently? What does hope like that feel like? How would you describe what it's like to hope?

For Hannah, this kind of hope felt like anguish, like deep pain. She would often go to God's house and cry bitter tears as she prayed to God for a child. If only He would grant her request!

One day, miraculously, God did just that. Here is what 1 Samuel 1:19–20 says:

> The LORD remembered her plea, and in due time she gave birth to a son. She named him Samuel, for she said, "I asked the LORD for him."

There is one phrase in that verse that I want you to notice: "in due time."

In due time, God responded to Hannah's request, and *in due time*, He always will respond to yours. He may not answer your heartfelt prayer in exactly the manner you expect, but *in due time*, He always will respond. Your hope is never, ever misplaced when that hope is placed in God. Romans 5:5 says, "And this hope will not lead to disappointment. For we know how dearly God loves us, because he has given us the Holy Spirit to fill our hearts with his love."

You are wise to keep hope alive.

Pause and Pray

God, I know what it's like to hope for things. To hope for a specific outcome. To hope for something I can see and touch. What's not as familiar to me is placing my hope in You. I'd like to try that today. Instead of hoping for something, I'd like to practice hoping in Someone . . . in You. Amen.

Reflect and Write

Matthew 12:21 says that "his name [the name of Jesus] will be the hope of all the world." How do you need for Jesus to be *your* hope today?

....

....

....

Steering Clear of Pain

Our strength grows out of our weakness.

RALPH WALDO EMERSON

What is your favorite animal? I've asked this question hundreds of times over the years, and most people respond with something like "dog," "cat," or "horse." Occasionally, I'll hear something like "river otter," "bearded dragon," or "rhinoceros." But mostly, people choose an animal that is lovable and loyal, smart and sweet, or really fast, really cool, or really strong.

You know what I've never once heard someone say in response to my favorite-animal question?

Sheep.

Nobody ever picks the sheep! And I think I know why. Yes, sheep can be cute, with their poofy hair and cloudlike bodies. But they're also dirty. They're stinky. They're loud. And (no offense) they're not the smartest animals on the planet. For instance, did you know that if one sheep walks right off the edge of a cliff, all the other sheep will likely follow it? Like I said, *not so smart.*

Which is why it can be a little upsetting to read verses like this one in the Bible: "You are my flock, the sheep of my pasture. You are my people, and I am your God" (Ezek. 34:31).

And this one: "Acknowledge that the Lord is God! He made us, and we are his. We are his people, the sheep of his pasture" (Ps. 100:3).

And this one: "All of us, like sheep, have strayed away. We have left God's paths to follow our own. Yet the Lord laid on him the sins of us all" (Isa. 53:6).

That's right. Out of all the animals God could have compared us to, He chose a sheep.

When I was a little girl, I prayed this bedtime prayer: "Jesus, gentle Shepherd, hear me / Bless Thy little lamb tonight / Through the darkness be Thou near me / Keep me safe 'til morning light." As I lay under a picture depicting Jesus holding a lamb, I was never completely sure if I was praying for the lamb or for me, but I prayed those words faithfully every night.

As it turns out, I *was* the lamb. And so are you.

We are weak and frail and helpless when it comes to running our own lives. We need a wise Shepherd to keep us on the path we're supposed to be on and to help us steer clear of danger and pain. And as we read in Psalm 23, God has given us just that:

> The Lord is my shepherd;
>   I have all that I need.
> He lets me rest in green meadows;
>   he leads me beside peaceful streams.
>   He renews my strength.
> He guides me along right paths,
>   bringing honor to his name.
> Even when I walk
>   through the darkest valley,

I will not be afraid,
 for you are close beside me.
Your rod and your staff
 protect and comfort me.
You prepare a feast for me
 in the presence of my enemies.
You honor me by anointing my head with oil.
 My cup overflows with blessings.
Surely your goodness and unfailing love will pursue me
 all the days of my life,
and I will live in the house of the LORD
 forever.

Yes, we may be sheep, but because of what God has done for us, we are well loved.

Pause and Pray

God, I admit that I'm not very good at running my own life. Like an impressionable little sheep, I tend to follow the crowd instead of doing what's best for me. Thanks for promising to lead me in the right direction and to protect me as a loving shepherd protects a flock. I love You, God! And I thank You for all the blessings You have given me in life. Amen.

Reflect and Write

Describe a time when you went your own way or fought for your own idea instead of asking God for wisdom and direction first. How might things have turned out differently if you had trusted God's guidance instead?

....

....

....

Spiritual Straight A's

True humility is not thinking less of yourself;
it is thinking of yourself less.

RICK WARREN

Once Jesus told a story about two people who were praying. Let's call the first person Self-righteous Sophie and the second one Humble Hope. In Jesus's story, Self-righteous Sophie stood all by herself and prayed, "Thank You, God, that I'm not as bad as other girls I know, girls who lie or cheat or steal. *I* always do the right thing. *I* always make great decisions. *I am* always amazing, through and through. If you were giving out grades for spiritual awesomeness, I bet I'd get straight A's."

Her prayer was basically a love letter—to herself. Yes, she followed all the rules, but her obedience didn't flow from a grateful heart. It flowed from her love for herself.

Then there was Humble Hope. Her prayer had a very different theme. "Oh, God," she said, "be merciful to me, because I make lots of mistakes. I mess up. I say the wrong things. I do the wrong things. I hurt the people I love. I'm really sorry for these things, and I definitely want to change. I know I can't change by myself.

Will *You* help me to change so that I can be a blessing to the people around me, so that I can live life looking more like You?"

After describing these two people praying, Jesus said this: "Those who exalt themselves will be humbled, and those who humble themselves will be exalted" (Luke 18:14). In other words, Jesus was saying, "My Father in heaven doesn't care about your spiritual straight A's. What He cares about is your honesty, your devotion, your *heart*."

I am sorry to say that I went through a season of life when I looked more like Sophie than Hope. I tried to keep all the rules so that God would be impressed with me. I wanted so badly for Him to like me that I worked like crazy to impress Him each day. I thought, *If I do everything perfectly, then God will love me and be happy with me.*

What I couldn't see then was that I didn't need to pile up good deeds for God; I simply needed to lay myself down.

The same is true for you. God *loves* you. Right now, He loves you completely, regardless of how "good" you've been today. And He will love you completely, regardless of what tomorrow holds.

Pause and Pray

God, I want to be like Humble Hope, a girl who has caught the idea of grace and who knows that she is completely loved. Help me to remember today that I don't have to pile up good deeds for You to accept and adore me. I just need to humble myself before You. Amen.

Reflect and Write

Who is a humble person you know? What makes them humble in your view? What could you learn from them?

. . . .

. . . .

. . . .

Me? Be Still?

Be still, and know that I am God!

PSALM 46:10

If you're like most people your age, your schedule is f-u-l-l, *full*. You carry a heavy class load at school, which means you have a load of homework each night. You are involved in sports or dance or church. Your weekends are stuffed with events. All this go, go, going can be really and truly fun. You love your friends. You love your classmates. You love your activities. You love your life. You love your church family. But the flip side is equally true: all that busyness can leave you feeling empty, exhausted, and alone.

I know how it is. My schedule is filled with different sorts of things these days, but every once in a while I feel the same way—empty, exhausted, and alone. Take earlier this year, for instance. Right in the midst of a swirling season of too many to-dos, my husband, Barry, and I were in a tiny town in Texas for a photo shoot. A photographer was going to take pictures of me to use for the cover of a new book I'd written. Barry and I had driven to a large barn in the country that is used as a wedding venue, and as I wandered through the main room, it took my breath away. This place was beautiful. Stunning, even. It had high ceilings and was flooded with natural light from the massive windows on all sides.

In the middle of the main room was the painted white chair that Barry had brought for me to sit on during the shoot, and as he continued to unload the car, I sensed an invitation that I knew was from God. "Come and sit for a while," He whispered to me.

And so I did. I walked over to the chair. I sat myself down. And I had a few quiet moments with the Lord. As I sat on that chair in the stillness of that space, everything else in my life took a back seat. For a few moments, all my cares, all my concerns, all my million-and-one things to do faded away, and it was just God and me and that chair.

Be still, and know that I am God!

That's what the psalmist says in Psalm 46:10. In the Message, the verse reads this way: "Step out of the traffic! Take a long, loving look at me, your High God, above politics, above everything." Being still on its own isn't enough. The real encouragement is found when we choose to be still . . . and to remember that God is God.

Pause and Pray

God, in the middle of all the things I need to do today, please give me the strength to stop and sit and be still in Your presence. Help me to make time to take a long, loving look at You. Help me to remember that You are bigger than all my busyness and that You really want to spend time with me. Amen.

Reflect and Write

What do you hope to see today when you take a long, loving look at God?

....

....

....

How Do I Look?

Which girl does Jesus love? This girl!

SHEILA WALSH

It's always fun to buy a new outfit, to slip on a pair of new shoes, to try a new hairstyle, to get a new shade of our favorite lip gloss, or to find a new scent of body lotion we love. But if we're not careful, we can put too much emphasis on having the "right" clothes or shoes, the "right" hairstyle, or the "right" brand of beauty products. We can start to believe that unless we have all these "right" things, we are somehow all wrong.

This happens because the world around us emphasizes these things. According to the world, we are what we wear. We are the products we use. We are how we look.

God says this just isn't true.

In 1 Samuel 16, God tells Samuel to go to a certain town and to find a man named Jesse, who lives there. "I have selected one of his sons to be my king," God explained, to which Samuel said, "How can I do that?" (vv. 1–2).

Samuel didn't want to make the *current* king mad by asking around for the guy who would be the new king. God told him He'd show him which person it was.

Later, when Samuel met Jesse's sons, he thought for sure that the first one was the one God wanted to be king. He was tall and handsome and seemed strong—perfect for a king, right?

But he wasn't the right man.

"Don't judge by his appearance or height," God said to Samuel, "for I have rejected him. The LORD doesn't see things the way you see them. People judge by outward appearance, but the LORD looks at the heart" (v. 7).

After God confirmed that none of the seven sons was the "chosen one," Samuel asked Jesse if he had any other children. Jesse's youngest son, a small-framed shepherd boy named David, was out in the fields tending to Jesse's flocks. David was brought in from the fields, and right away Samuel knew that he was the one.

Regardless of how David looked on the outside—his youth, his height, his job—God saw a king. He saw a noble leader, a world changer.

Do you want to know a secret? When God looks at you, He sees a girl He loves. He sees someone who is brave and strong, who is loving and caring, who is special and smart. He sees His beloved daughter.

The question that remains is this: Will you choose to see yourself this way too?

Pause and Pray

God, sometimes when I think about myself, I think negative thoughts—what could be better, what could look better, how I could improve. I don't always think about words like "brave" and "loving" and "special" and "smart." Thank You for reminding me that You don't see me the same way the world sees me . . . or the way I see myself. You see me from the inside out. What You see when You look at me is not my body or my face but my heart. Amen.

Reflect and Write

What do you like about yourself that you can thank God for today?

....

....

....

Mean Girl in My Head

If you want to change how you act, you
have to change how you think.

SHEILA WALSH

What are you thinking about right now?

And right now?

How about now?

Experts estimate that we think between fifty thousand and eighty thousand thoughts per day, which is roughly three thousand thoughts per hour. This means that in a given minute, we have fifty thoughts, which is a little less than one thought per second. We're thinking *machines*, which is a fantastic thing. Thinking or reasoning is what sets us apart from other animals. We have minds. We have ideas. Which is great, except for this: not all of those thoughts are good thoughts.

People who study these things tell us that of the sixty-five thousand thoughts (on average) we think in a day, roughly 80 percent of them are negative. This means that for every ten thoughts we think, *eight* of them aren't helpful. *Eight* of them sound like this:

"You're not enough."

"This is never going to work."

"You're not doing it right."

"Everything is going wrong."

"You're a failure."

"Nobody likes you."

"Why did you say that?"

"Why did you do that?"

"Why can't you ever get it right?"

Sigh. This is bad news. Are you ready for some news that is *good*? How about this: you can tell your brain what to think. You can tell the mean girl in your head to go home.

If you're ready for some good thoughts, some better thoughts, some productive thoughts that are straight from the heart of God to you, then the next time a negative thought comes to mind, choose to think one of these thoughts instead:

- God loves me with an everlasting love. (Jer. 31:3)
- I am God's masterpiece, and He has created me for good works. (Eph. 2:10)
- God delights in the details of my life. (Ps. 37:23)

Just for one minute—sixty simple seconds—choose to tell your brain what to think instead of letting your thoughts take control of you. And when the next minute shows up, make the same choice again.

Pause and Pray

*God, what a gift it is that I can choose what to think about!
Please help me to think positive thoughts today. Amen.*

Reflect and Write

What is one positive thought you will choose to carry with you
throughout this day?

....

....

....

Worst Movie Ever

Delete the files. God has!

———

SHEILA WALSH

What's the best movie you've ever seen? I polled a few of my younger friends, and here are some movies that landed at the top of the list: *Frozen*, *The Greatest Show-man*, *Lord of the Rings*. I didn't ask those same people about the *worst* movie they'd ever seen, but I'm sure those answers would have been interesting too.

Now, what do you think would happen if I told the people I polled that for the next year they had to watch not their favorite movie but their *least* favorite movie, every single day?

Do you think they'd sign up for a job like that?

Of course not! If someone hates a movie, why would they watch it twice, let alone *three hundred and sixty-five times*? Why would anyone subject themselves to such an ordeal?

And yet that is exactly what we do whenever we hang on to mistakes we've made, replaying them over and over in our minds. They are like a bad movie we keep pushing Play on.

Day . . . after day . . . after day.

Thankfully, we can choose another way. In Psalm 103:12, we read this:

> He [God] has removed our sins as far from us
> as the east is from the west.

In other words, once we ask God to forgive us, He places our worst movies as far away from us as possible. He sticks them waaaay over there. Out of arm's reach. Not only that, but He remembers them no more. So why should we?

Pause and Pray

God, thank You for not punishing me for the mistakes I make. Thank You for not dealing harshly with me by reminding me again and again of all I've done wrong. Thank You for putting my sins far, far away from me and for welcoming me with open arms even after I've goofed up. Amen.

Reflect and Write

What mistake/goof/sin do you need to quit replaying in your mind? Decide today to quit pushing Play on that movie.

....

....

....

Uncomfortable

Your promise revives me;
it comforts me in all my troubles.

PSALM 119:50

When something makes our bodies uncomfortable, we can usually do something about it. We can cut the tag out of our shirt. We can put on an extra layer when we're cold. We can scratch an itch. But what do we do when our *souls* are uncomfortable . . . when we're uncomfortable on the *inside*?

To scratch a "soul" itch, you could turn to *distractions*. You could scroll social media. You could play hours and hours of video games. You could watch makeup tutorials on YouTube.

You could turn to *food*. You could eat an entire bag of gummy worms. A whole box of Whoppers. Bowl after bowl of Lucky Charms or ice cream or chips.

You could turn to *productivity*, trying to organize or clean or perform your way out of the discomfort you feel.

You could turn to any number of things to try to relieve the soul discomfort you're experiencing, but only one thing will truly help. In 2 Corinthians 1:3, the apostle Paul refers to God as "the source of all comfort." He then says this:

> He [God] comforts us in all our troubles so that we can comfort others. When they are troubled, we will be able to give them the same comfort God has given us. (v. 4)

Do you see it? When you are uncomfortable on the inside, find a quiet place and ask God to comfort you. Tell Him everything you are feeling. Not only will you find comfort for your soul, but you will also be able to share that comfort with those you love.

Pause and Pray

God, I know what it's like to feel uncomfortable on the inside, the kind of discomfort that games and snacks just can't resolve. Thank You for promising to comfort me when I feel that way and for using me to bring comfort to my friends. Amen.

Reflect and Write

Do you know someone who needs some soul-level comfort? How might you help bring comfort to them today?

....

....

....

Label Maker

See how very much our Father loves us, for he
calls us his children, and that is what we are!

1 JOHN 3:1

These days it seems like everyone has a label, and those labels
usually aren't nice.

weird	depressed
ugly	annoying
stupid	unwanted
unloved	angry
useless	broken
not cool	

Ugh. Such awful labels, right? Maybe you've been labeled with
certain words along the way and have names you could add to that
list. Have you ever been called "the difficult one" or "the weird
one"? On the other end of the spectrum, maybe you've been called
"smart" or "mature" or "pretty" only to feel stuck in a box you can't
get out of. If you're supposed to be "the smart one," for instance,
what happens when you don't get a perfect grade? If you're known
as "the pretty one," what happens when a pimple shows up? Can
"the mature one" ever have a bad day?

These types of labels are unhelpful because they either hold you to an impossible standard or keep you from reaching the potential that is yours. It is far better to let God label you instead. In 1 John 1:3, God calls you His.

See how very much our Father loves us, for he calls us his children, and that is what we are!

His label maker has been busy since the beginning of time labeling women and men and girls and boys and tweens and teens with labels that are helpful instead. Want to know what His labels say?

precious	bought with a price
beloved	adored
redeemed	beautiful
forgiven	priceless
seen	gifted
accepted	Mine

Let those labels be the only labels that stick to you. Trash the other labels for good!

Pause and Pray

God, I commit to defining myself according to how You define me. Help me to label myself with only positive, life-giving, truth-based labels today. Amen.

Reflect and Write

Which labels will you choose to wear today? Circle three from the good-labels list above, and use the following lines to explain why you chose them.

....

....

....

You Can't Make Me

Respect everyone, and love the family of believers.

———————

1 PETER 2:17

I remember when I was about your age getting upset with my mom because I had to be in bed at least an hour before my friends on Saturday night. It seemed so unfair. I sat on my bed thinking, *You can't make me*, but then I realized I was sitting on my bed. I guess she could!

Do you ever get frustrated with your parents? What about your teachers and coaches when they tell you something that hurts your feelings or that you don't agree with? How about other authority figures you encounter? Sometimes people your age have an attitude of disrespect, like I did when I thought, *You can't make me*. Let me suggest another way, an attitude of gratitude and surrender: "Thanks for looking out for me!"

God has a specific opinion on these things. In 1 Timothy 2:1–2, we read these words:

Pray for all people. Ask God to help them; intercede on their behalf, and give thanks for them. Pray this way for kings and all who are in authority so that we can live peaceful and quiet lives marked by godliness and dignity.

It's easy to think we know better than the people in authority over us—parents and teachers and coaches and all the rest. We see this attitude every day on television or at school. But God tells us not to take the easy way out here. He tells us instead to *pray* for our parents. To *pray* for our teachers. To *pray* for the leaders of our country.

So let me ask you, When was the last time you prayed for the people who have authority in your life? What might happen—in your heart, in your relationships with those people, even in *their* lives—if you were to decide *never* to criticize or disrespect them? I know this can be hard sometimes when life doesn't seem fair, but God will honor your commitment to honor His Word.

Pause and Pray

God, I can see that You have put certain people in my life to help me grow up, become mature, and learn to love well. I want to treat those people well. I don't want to have a critical spirit toward them. Instead, I want to be kind toward them. Appreciative. Service oriented. Grateful. I want to let go of a judgmental attitude and pray for them instead. Please help me to do so. Amen.

Reflect and Write

Which of the authority figures in your life can you thank God for today? A parent? A coach? A teacher? A leader in your community? Someone else? Write out a prayer of thanksgiving for that person now.

....

....

....

False Advertising

There is great freedom in telling the truth.

SHEILA WALSH

Anna's mom was standing at the bottom of the stairs. "Anna, did you get your room cleaned?" she hollered.

Anna knew why she was asking. Anna's friends were waiting at the front door for her to go sledding with them, but Anna's mom had told her she couldn't go until her room was picked up. Clearly, her mom didn't understand just how much work there was to do. Clothes from the week that had never quite gotten hung back up littered the floor. A confetti spray of paper bedding surrounded Anna's guinea pig cage. Art supplies that Anna had neglected to gather back up made her bed look like a craft store explosion. This place was a *mess*.

Anna stood in the center of the chaos and surveyed the scene. As she exhaled her exasperation, an idea came to mind. Trudging through the river of jeans and sweatshirts and shoes, she made it to the other side of the room. She opened the closet door wide, turned back toward the disaster, and then, like a bulldozer, pushed every last ounce of clutter into her closet—including the guinea pig, whose eyes were now wide with concern. Pushing as hard as she could, she got the closet door shut, she dusted off her hands, and she nodded satisfaction at her spotless room.

"Yeah, Mom!" Anna hollered as she grabbed her snow pants and flew down the stairs. "All clean!"

By the time Anna returned from sledding, her mom had discovered her deception. "Sweetie," her mom began, "your guinea pig was squealing so loudly that I thought she was in real trouble. You can imagine my surprise when I found her in your closet . . . underneath a mountain of other stuff."

"Uh, yeah . . . about that," Anna said. "I was going to clean all that stuff up for real, but I didn't have time . . ."

Anna tried several times to justify herself, but even she knew that what she'd done was wrong. "I'd better get changed and work on my room now," she finally said as she gave her mom a quick hug and headed for the stairs.

"Yes," her mom said. "And next time let's be sure your 'Yeah, Mom, all clean!' is sincere."

In Matthew 5:37, Jesus says this:

Don't say anything you don't mean. . . . Just say "yes" and "no." When you manipulate words to get your own way, you go wrong. (Message)

Thankfully, we don't have to go wrong.

Pause and Pray

God, today may my yes be yes and my no be no. I want to be a person who says what she means and means what she says. By Your power, I know I can be. Amen.

Reflect and Write

What emotion do you think you'll experience when you tell the *whole* truth today?

....

....

....

Honestly?

Tell God what you really feel, not what
you think you're supposed to feel.

SHEILA WALSH

H ave you ever told God what you really feel, what you really think? Sometimes we think we're supposed to say the "right" things to God even if we don't feel them. At times we do that with our friends and our families too. We don't know how they will react, so we try to protect ourselves.

We lie to put ourselves in a better light. We lie to protect people's feelings. We lie to escape punishment for something we shouldn't have done. We lie to keep friends' secrets safe.

While we may never live in a world where people always tell the truth, there is one place we can go where it's always safe to do so. The presence of God.

If you've ever read the book of Psalms, then you know that the people who wrote those psalms were *really* comfortable being honest with God. They screamed if they felt outraged. They howled if they needed a good cry. They laughed when they were happy. They praised God when life went right. Sometimes they did all those things in *one* psalm! See if you can spot the different emotions in Psalm 43:

> Clear my name, God; stick up for me
> against these loveless, immoral people.

Get me out of here, away
>from these lying degenerates.
I counted on you, God.
>Why did you walk out on me?
Why am I pacing the floor, wringing my hands
>over these outrageous people?
Give me your lantern and compass,
>give me a map,
so I can find my way to the sacred mountain,
>to the place of your presence,
to enter the place of worship,
>meet my exuberant God,
sing my thanks with a harp,
>magnificent God, my God.
Why are you down in the dumps, dear soul?
>Why are you crying the blues?
Fix my eyes on God—
>soon I'll be praising again.
He puts a smile on my face.
>He's my God. (Message)

You can ask God to stick up for you when you feel like no one else is. You can express anger to God when you feel like He's been unfair. You can beg God for wisdom when you don't know which way to go. You can tell Him exactly how you're feeling every single time, knowing He won't turn His back on you. He can handle your fear. He can handle your disappointment. He can handle your questions. He can handle your pain. God can handle your truth—whatever it is. You can pour out your heart to Him.

Pause and Pray

God, I want to trust You with the truth of what's going on with me—in my mind, in my heart, in my life. Thank You for promising to accept me no matter how I'm truly feeling. Thank You for loving me still. Amen.

Reflect and Write

What secret can you confide in God today? How do you hope He will respond?

....

....

....

PART 3

Telling

the Truth

———

God longs to speak truth over the lies we tell ourselves—
that we're not enough, that we don't please Him, that we'll
never make it in life.

As we sit and talk with Him, He exposes
those false beliefs and overpowers them
with the truth.

———

Trusted Friend

A friend is someone who knows all
about you and loves you still.

SHEILA WALSH

Who are your besties, the friends you couldn't do life without? A few of my best friends I've known for decades, and every time we're together I think, *I would hate to think of how much joy I'd miss without these friends in my life.*

We love to laugh. We love to take walks. We love to talk about life. We love to just hang out. Each one of them is such a gift to me. I pray I'm a gift in their lives too.

Two of those friends are actually relatives of mine—my husband, Barry, and Christian, my son. Barry and I have been married for twenty-six years and have had some serious ups and downs along the way, but this much I know: I love him more today than I did when I said yes to being his wife back in 1994—long before you were even born!

My son, Christian, is twenty-three years old now, but I remember on the day of his birth thinking that something inside me had utterly and completely changed. I was a *mother* now. And the love I had for that little boy was different from any other love I'd known. Still today my love for Christian is special. I absolutely adore my son.

But despite all these deep emotions I hold for my husband, my son, and my other best friends, there is one relationship that is sweeter still: my relationship with Jesus. He really is the best of my bests. And the good news is that not only do I consider Him my friend, but He also thinks of me that way too. Here is what John 15:15 says:

> Now you are my friends, since I have told you everything the Father told me.

I'm sure that when God sees our earthly friendships, He delights in those loving bonds. But when we think of our closest friend, our best of the bests, He wants us to think of His Son.

Human friendships can bring lots of happiness to our lives, but humans are flawed. Our friends and family members won't *always* be delightful. They won't *always* be able to help us. They won't *always* be there when we need them.

No, if we're looking for someone who will never fail us, we need to look to Jesus. He will never leave us. He will never forsake us. He will never betray our trust. He is the friend of all friends, the best of the best. He's the One we can't do without.

Pause and Pray

God, thank You for the gift of my besties here on earth. They bring so much comfort and joy to my life. And thank You for the gift of Your friendship and for promising never to leave my side. Amen.

Reflect and Write

What qualities do you most value in a friend? How does Jesus bring those qualities to life?

....

....

....

Never Insecure

I left my overcoat of shame at the foot of the cross.

SHEILA WALSH

What makes you feel insecure? Maybe you feel insecure about speaking in front of a group. (You wouldn't be the only one to feel that way. The smart people who study fear say that most people fear public speaking more than they fear even death!)

Maybe you feel insecure about your athletic abilities . . . or lack thereof. You dread the team sports unit in PE at school because you just know you'll drop the ball. (Literally . . . that was me!)

Maybe you feel insecure about talking with people you don't know. Or about asking questions in class. Or about memorizing facts for a test.

Maybe you feel insecure about how you look . . . that's one I can definitely relate to. Specifically, I don't like having photographs taken, which is why I can stand in front of a giant crowd of people and tell them about Jesus with no fear, but if you stick me in a photo shoot, I'm not so relaxed. I *really* don't like having my picture taken. I feel goofy standing and grinning at the camera while being told to look "natural." Maybe you can relate. School pictures anyone?

Everyone has something about themselves they're insecure about. But if we're not careful, we can start to fixate on that thing. We can start to think that our value lies in that imperfect part of us, which means we must not be very valuable at all. We can start to feel ashamed of ourselves, of how God made us, of how we *are*. And then we can wear that shame like a coat, all day, every day, everywhere we go. We can let our whole life be overtaken by that one thing we don't prefer and miss the beautiful life God has in store for us.

In Revelation 5:11–12, the song the angels sing together is this one:

> Then I looked again, and I heard the voices of thousands and millions of angels around the throne and of the living beings and the elders. And they sang in a mighty chorus:
>
> > "Worthy is the Lamb who was slaughtered—
> > > to receive power and riches
> > and wisdom and strength
> > > and honor and glory and blessing."

Do you want to know what I do any time I feel insecure? I remember this powerful truth: because I have tucked myself into Jesus's care, His worthiness covers me.

It's true for you too. If you have surrendered your heart to Jesus, then because He is worthy, you are worthy as well. You and I never again have to believe the lies that insecurity tells us. We can find our worthiness not in how we look or how fast we can run or how we engage with strangers or whether we can wow a crowd but rather in Him alone.

Because He is worthy, you are worthy.

Pause and Pray

God, the pressures of this world sure can make a person feel insecure! I'm so glad to be reminded that I am worthy in Your sight! I don't have to let insecure thoughts run unchecked through my head. I can stop them and send them right back. I can choose to see worthiness in the mirror each day. Amen.

Reflect and Write

What lies about yourself might go away if you truly believe you are worthy just as you are?

....

....

....

Holy Place

Prayer used to be on my to-do list.
Now it's on my who-I-am list.

O ne morning I couldn't find my husband. Plus, my dogs, Maggie and Tink, were barking their heads off for no apparent reason. It was barely 7:00 a.m. Barry had gone missing, and my dogs had gone crazy. Not a good start to the day.

I headed downstairs hollering Barry's name, and finally I heard a muffled response. "Morning!" he said from the depths of our closet beneath our staircase. The dogs had found Barry first, and he was hip deep in boxes, blankets, and Christmas ornaments—all the stuff we kept in that closet. "What are you doing?" I asked him, to which he said, "I'm clearing out all this junk . . . to make a *prayer closet*."

He said the words "prayer closet" reverently, in something like the hushed voice you use in a library.

The next few days Barry learned the hard way that when you close the door to that particular closet, no light can get in, making it very hard to read your Bible. He learned that when you try to use candles for light in there, you catch everything on fire. And he learned that if you stand up too fast from the floor of your beloved prayer closet, you bonk your head on the bottom of the staircase that sits atop that room.

He also learned that if you stay in your dark, quiet prayer closet a little too long, your "prayer time" turns into a nap.

In the end, my darling husband's prayer-closet experiment failed. But thankfully, God doesn't need us to outfit any special rooms to meet with Him in prayer. Second Corinthians 6:16 says this:

> I will live in them
>   and walk among them.
> I will be their God,
>   and they will be my people.

He is eager to talk with us anytime, any day, wherever we are, whatever we're doing, about anything, and for as long as we want.

In the shower.

While we're getting dressed.

In the car.

On the bus.

In school.

As we walk the dog.

While we wait in line.

While we eat.

While we brush our teeth.

Just after we climb into bed.

Anywhere.

Everywhere.

God is there . . . and there . . . and there—and so very eager to talk with us.

Pause and Pray

God, I don't understand how You can hear all the prayers of all Your people at all times throughout the day, but I'm so glad You can. I love knowing that I can come into Your presence anytime and anywhere. I don't need a special room. I don't need special clothing. I don't need fancy words. I just need what's already here—my mind, my heart, my questions, my concerns, my praise, and my devotion to You. Amen.

Reflect and Write

Think about all the places you will be today. What would happen if you decided now to talk with God in each of those spots?

....

....

....

Powerful

Prayer activates the power of God.

SHEILA WALSH

At last count, there were seventeen billion connected devices in the world. That means, on average, each person on earth has two to three devices in use—smartphones and smart watches and e-readers and laptops and more. By the end of 2020, that number is expected to climb to more than twenty billion. That's a lot of devices! And guess what all those devices need?

Power.

If you want to strike fear into the hearts of most people alive today, just tell them that their charging cord has gone missing. This news will make them *freak out*. Why? Because without power, those devices are useless. And without our phones, won't we all die? (Just kidding!)

Ephesians 1:19–20 says this:

I also pray that you will understand the incredible greatness of God's power for us who believe him. This is the same mighty power that raised Christ from the dead and seated him in the place of honor at God's right hand in the heavenly realms.

As is true with our favorite devices, if we don't "charge up" in power, our usefulness will be greatly compromised.

We must look to God for the power we need to live a life that pleases Him, the same power that raised Christ from the dead.

So how do we access the power we desire? You got it: it happens through prayer. Prayer activates the power of God.

If you want to be powerful, you'll stay plugged into prayer.

Pause and Pray

God, if people only knew where real power was found, they'd be praying all day, every day! You hold all power in the palm of Your hand, and You promise to share that power with those who seek You, who surrender to You, who look for ways to serve others instead of spending all their energy fighting for their own way. Thank You for reminding me that I need to stay charged up through prayer. Amen.

Reflect and Write

What do you think the difference is between the power the world seeks and the power God provides?

....

....

....

God Is Near

The LORD is close to all who call on him,
yes, to all who call on him in truth.

PSALM 145:18

I travel to Africa a couple times each year, setting up feeding programs in schools and working with our team to put water wells in villages where there is no clean water source. One thing I learned very quickly is that you must dress right if you don't want unwelcome visitors such as large bugs, poisonous frogs, or scaly snakes climbing up your legs. There are all sorts of things scampering around out there, and they're all things I don't want jumping on me!

On these trips, my group and I stay not in a fancy hotel but in the bush—in the most remote parts of the most remote villages there are. When we get to a new village, we ask the village chief for permission to camp there. Once we've met all the village elders and have received their blessing, we set up our tents for the night.

You will never see the stars as clearly as you do in Africa. Where we camp, there is no electricity, no lights from a town or from cars, so after the sun goes down and the fire we've cooked over goes out, the sky lights up with the most magnificent display you've ever seen. It's breathtaking.

My son asked me after I got home from one of these trips if I ever felt lonely or scared so far away from home. I thought about his question for a bit. The truth is that when all the noise of our world is gone, when the distraction of television and social media is quiet, I am so aware of the presence of God. As I look up at the stars, I remember the promise God gave to Abraham that his descendants would be as numerous as the stars. In Africa, I see what Abraham saw, God's magnificent art show on display. It's so humbling to remember that the God who put all the stars and planets in place sees you and me, that He never leaves us, that He is right here with us now.

Hebrews 13:5 puts it this way:

For God has said,
    "I will never fail you.
        I will never abandon you."

The Lord is always at hand. You are never alone. He's here. He sees. He cares.

Pause and Pray

God, I love the idea that You are always with me. You really are near, before and behind me, to my left and to my right. Thank You for sticking close to me even when I don't realize You're there. Give me eyes to see You, Father. May I be quick to acknowledge Your presence. Amen.

Reflect and Write

What does God's presence feel like to you? How would you describe it to a friend who had never experienced it before?

....

....

....

Truth and Freedom

Honesty is the first chapter in the book of wisdom.

THOMAS JEFFERSON

Years ago, the movie *Liar Liar* came out, which featured a dad who always told lies. He lied at work. He lied at home. He lied to his friends. He lied to his enemies. He even lied to his wife and young son. Everyone was hurt by this guy's lies, but still he lied and lied. One day after being stood up yet again by his dad, the son made a wish. He wished that for just twenty-four hours his dad couldn't tell a lie. Amazingly, the boy's wish came true.

The movie takes many hilarious twists and turns from that point forward, revealing just how different his life was because he could no longer tell even a fib. For example, when the dad is pulled over by a policeman for speeding, instead of saying, "I'm so sorry, officer, but I had no idea I was going so fast!" he says, "I sped. I followed too closely. I ran a stop sign. I almost hit a Chevy. I sped some more. I failed to yield at a crosswalk. I changed lanes at the intersection. I changed lanes without signaling while running a red light and speeding!"

The officer looks as perplexed as your parents probably would if when you were told to stop pestering your little brother you said, "Mom. Dad. I was wrong. I knowingly bothered him. I knew I was bugging him, but I refused to stop, because, well, I was enjoying watching him be bothered. I am guilty. This is totally my fault. I deserve whatever punishment is coming my way, because this one is *all* on me."

The temptation, whenever we're caught doing something wrong, is to defend ourselves and rattle off all the reasons or excuses why we're absolutely not at fault. And yet if we want to grow in spiritual maturity, we simply have to risk coming clean. Look at the words of Psalm 139:23–24:

> Search me, O God, and know my heart;
>> test me and know my anxious thoughts.
> Point out anything in me that offends you,
>> and lead me along the path of everlasting life.

David prayed this prayer after he did something terribly wrong. It was a hard prayer to pray, but it brought him freedom and forgiveness.

Praying a prayer like that takes great courage! It requires dropping our defensiveness, opening our lives wide open, and asking God to show us every last thing He would change. Doing this might be hard, but it will set us free.

Pause and Pray

God, I beg You for the courage to pray these words and to mean them: I invite You to search me, to know my heart, and to untangle my anxious thoughts. I ask You to show me anything that doesn't please You . . . anything at all! The last thing I want to do is hold on tight to something that hurts Your heart. Show me the problem areas, and then please help me to fix them. Amen.

Reflect and Write

Ask God to show you a problem area in your life. Then record what you sense Him saying in response. What would He have you change?

....

....

....

Hearing from God

> I assume that the Spirit is always whispering
> "Abba" to God's children, assuring them
> that they are safe in his care.
>
> ———
>
> LARRY CRABB

As the story goes, one night a young boy who lived inside a place of worship heard the priest call his name. "Samuel, Samuel!" the voice called, waking the boy up.

The boy rushed to the priest's bedroom. "Yes, sir?" the boy asked. But the priest was fast asleep.

"Hmmm," the boy muttered as he made his way back to his room.

Just as the boy was getting settled under his comfy blankets, he heard the voice again. "Samuel, Samuel!"

Samuel ran to the priest's room a second time but again found the priest sound asleep.

What is going on here? the boy wondered. *Who keeps calling my name?*

A third time the voice called, "Samuel!" A third time Samuel rushed down the hallway. A third time the priest was asleep.

Who was calling Samuel's name? If you think it was God, you are right.

The third time, having been awakened by Samuel's voice, the priest looked at the boy and said, "Go and lie down again, and if someone calls again, say, 'Speak, LORD, your servant is listening'" (1 Sam. 3:9).

I love this story from the Old Testament because it reminds me that God loves to speak to His followers and that God speaks to kids! Think of it: God might speak to *you* today; He might call *your* name.

He might speak to you through the Bible. He might speak to you through a wise person you know. He might speak to you through nature. He might speak to you through a prompting He gives you in prayer. However He chooses to speak to you, I imagine the message He conveys will be sweet. "I see you," He might say.

"I love you."

"I care for you."

"You are safe."

"You are treasured."

"You are delightful."

"You are beloved."

"Grace is yours."

Pause and Pray

God, more than anything else I want today, I want to hear from You. Open my ears so that when You call my name, I will respond as quickly as Samuel did. Help me to lean in and listen for You. Amen.

Reflect and Write

Whether or not you could hear Him audibly, do you think God has ever spoken to you before? What sort of message did He convey? What did you do in response?

....

....

....

Praying for Pants

With God on our side like this, how can we lose?

ROMANS 8:31 MESSAGE

My father passed away when I was just a little girl, and after his death, my family lived in a poor part of town in housing provided by the government. My mom made very little money, and while my siblings and I received free meals at school because of our financial situation, we still had to wear the right school uniform every day.

One night near the end of a semester, my mom told us to gather around her chair. "We're going to pray," she said, which wasn't all that unusual coming from her. Evidently, my brother had hit a growth spurt, and now his school pants were way too short. We didn't have the money to buy new ones, and Mom didn't want him getting into trouble at school. She told us that it was time to pray for some pants!

I was young at the time, and after Mom finished her prayer for my brother's pants, I wondered if some new trousers would somehow magically come flying down the chimney, as if God kept spare pairs in heaven. *How is God going to give my brother pants?* I wondered. This was more than my mind could conceive of.

A few days later, a family friend came over to have tea with my mom, and as she stood up to leave, she set a package on the couch. After she'd gone, my mom opened the box to find three pairs of pants inside, all in my brother's size. "Did you tell her about our need?" I asked my mother, to which she said, "No. But we told the Lord."

Romans 8:31–32 says this:

With God on our side like this, how can we lose? If God didn't hesitate to put everything on the line for us, embracing our condition and exposing himself to the worst by sending his own Son, is there anything else he wouldn't gladly and freely do for us? (Message)

If I have learned anything since my childhood days, it's that God really does want what is best for us and really can be trusted to meet our needs. Yes, there have been times when my list of prayer requests didn't line up with His perfect timing, but even then God proved Himself faithful to care for me in my need.

Do you look to God for the needs you face, even for things that seem too trivial for prayer? He is near, and He is listening. What might you trust Him to provide right now?

Pause and Pray

God, sometimes I think You are way too busy to be bothered with my simple requests. I don't want to bug You. And yet these needs are bugging me! Teach me to trust You with my big decisions and complications . . . and also with ones that are small. Amen.

Reflect and Write

What small provision can you trust God for today?

....

....

....

New Mercy Every Day

Where mercy, love, and pity dwell,
there God is dwelling too.

WILLIAM BLAKE

What is your morning routine like? Do you wake up to an alarm clock or a parent's voice telling you it's time to get out of bed? You probably go to the bathroom soon after waking. And then maybe you get dressed and brush your teeth and eat breakfast. Or maybe you eat breakfast and then brush your teeth and then get dressed. Do you drink a glass of water? Feed a pet? Gather your books and stuff them into your backpack? Do you have time to sit and talk with a family member or read a book or text a friend?

Most everyone I know has what they call a "morning routine." In my friend group, that routine usually involves coffee. And putting on workout clothes, despite the fact that we rarely *actually* work out. And spending time with our spouses or taking the dogs for a walk. That routine also involves *spiritual* disciplines, such as sitting quietly, reading Scripture, capturing thoughts in a journal, and praying.

I've always loved a passage found in the Old Testament. Lamentations 3:22–23 goes like this:

> The faithful love of the LORD never ends!
>> His mercies never cease.
> Great is his faithfulness;
>> his mercies begin afresh each morning.

That last line has brought me great comfort over the years: "his mercies begin afresh each morning." Another translation calls those mercies "new." Think of it. Each morning as you wake up and get going with your day, a grand reset button in heaven has been pushed, and God's mercies have been made new. His willingness to accept you and forgive you and pursue you and be with you . . . all of that desire has been refreshed. And today, on this new day, according to Scripture, God says, "My tanks are full! Come and take whatever you need!"

So here is what I'm thinking. Beginning today, why don't we add one more thing to our morning routine? Let's look for God's mercy each day. Just as God provided manna for the Israelites each morning so they could eat, He provides mercy for us today. Between eating our breakfast and brushing our teeth (or vice versa, if that's how you roll), let's ask God to show us His fresh supply of mercy. Let's make that the most important part of our morning routine.

Pause and Pray

God, it blows my mind to think that every time I wake up, a brand-new supply of divine mercy is waiting for me. Thank You, Father, for being so compassionate and caring. Help me to see—and highly value—Your fresh mercy today. Amen.

Reflect and Write

What's the most challenging part of your mornings these days? How might your mornings improve if you try to spot God's new mercy each day?

....

....

....

A Shoulder to Cry On

For I hold you by your right hand—
I, the LORD your God.
And I say to you,
"Don't be afraid. I am here to help you."

ISAIAH 41:13

Just before Jesus faced His awful death on a cross, He took His closest friends into a garden and asked them to keep watch while He prayed. He was in agony. He knew what lay ahead, and honestly, He didn't want any part of it. But He trusted His Father's will, saying, "Please take this cup of suffering away from me. Yet I want your will to be done, not mine" (Mark 14:36).

In the Gospel of Luke, we learn that Jesus was so distressed over His coming crucifixion that He started sweating drops of *blood*.

I imagine Jesus kneeling in prayer, His mind reeling and His heart breaking, His body utterly shutting down. He wants to do what God wants Him to do, but does that have to involve something like *this*?

It's a devastating scene. And also a helpful one. Here's why. There will come a time (or there has already) when you will be so sad, so upset, so distraught that you won't know what to do. You'll feel like your world is unraveling, and you'll have no idea which way to turn. You'll have made a huge mistake or someone you love will have hurt you so badly or some other awful thing will have unfolded, and you'll sit there in your bed feeling like life as you know it is over. In that moment, I want you to think of Jesus in the garden of Gethsemane, beads of blood dotting His forehead.

Hebrews 4:15 says:

This High Priest of ours understands our weaknesses, for he faced all of the same testings we do, yet he did not sin.

Not only does Jesus see you and love you, but He also understands the pain you're in. What's more, He knows how to help you work through things that feel unbearable because He worked through unbearable things of His own.

Some things are way too hard to face on your own. When those times come, turn to Jesus. He has been there. He knows what to do.

Pause and Pray

God, only You understand what it's like to be in true agony, and only You can help me when an agonizing situation unfolds. Help me to remember this truth for future reference. On that day, help me to look to You. Amen.

Reflect and Write

How does it make you feel to know that Jesus understands the full range of your deepest emotions and that He experienced them all Himself?

....

....

....

Heavenly Bottle

Heaven catches every silent tear.

SHEILA WALSH

It feels good when someone remembers a struggle and asks you about it later. If you run into a friend you haven't seen in a few days and she remembers that you recently suffered a gymnastics injury, it feels good to have her ask, "How is your wrist feeling?"

If you return to school after having been gone for a few days to attend a funeral, it feels good to have your teacher say, "We sure missed you while you were away. I'm so sorry to hear about the loss of your grandfather."

When people remember our pain, it feels honoring. It feels comforting. It feels *good*. And while we can't expect friends and teachers and family members to always remember, Scripture tells us that God always does. Psalm 56:8 says this:

> You [God] keep track of all my sorrows.
> You have collected all my tears in your bottle.
> You have recorded each one in your book.

Several years ago, a friend gave me a gift, a beautiful cobalt-blue bottle. It was tiny—just two or three inches tall—and it was covered in silver filigree . . . stunning. At first I thought it was a perfume bottle, but then I found the note she had included with the gift. She had bought the bottle during a trip to Israel, and it was a "tear" bottle.

In the days of Jesus, bottles just like my blue one were used to catch the tears of people walking to a graveyard to bury a loved one. The tears were a visible symbol of how dearly the deceased person was loved. Evidently, the more tears that were collected, the more valued the person was said to be.

Which makes perfect sense, given what the psalmist says is true for you and me: God collects *all* our tears in His bottle; not a single tear we cry is shed in vain. Every time we have suffered, He has noticed. Every tear matters deeply to Him.

Pause and Pray

God, I can't tell you how comforting it is to know that I never cry alone and that I never cry in vain. You always see. You always care. You always remember my pain. Amen.

Reflect and Write

How does it help you to know that God has a bottle waiting to catch every tear you cry?

....

....

....

Accepted

Grace is God's accepting of us. Faith is our
acceptance of God accepting us.

ADRIAN ROGERS

———

The summer I turned eighteen I volunteered at a drop-in center for senior citizens in my hometown of Ayr, on the west coast of Scotland. Basically, people in their later years of life would come to the center for several hours at a time to relax; read; work on a craft; or play board games, card games, or dominoes. My role was to be their friend, bring them coffee and snacks, and serve them lunch. I listened to their stories. I played games with them. I helped them have a good time. And for the most part, the people I met there were kind and fun loving and happy to see me each time.

The one exception was a man who always sat away from the rest of the group, in the back corner of the room, arms folded against his chest. He'd never come to the table for lunch, so I made a practice of taking him his food on a tray. One day I pulled up a chair beside him and sat there quietly as he ate. He didn't seem to want to chat, but I felt bad leaving him to eat all alone. So I sat. I waited. I stared off into the distance as he chewed.

On day ten, he finally spoke. "I'm an American!" he said gruffly.

"That's awesome," I said. "I hope to visit there someday."

He softened. "If you ever get to Poughkeepsie, will you please tell them George says hi?"

I had no idea what Poughkeepsie was, but I agreed I would. (Years later, I did make it to America. I did go to Poughkeepsie. And with as much passion as I could muster, I shouted to no one in particular, "George says hi!")

Back at the senior center, every day following that day, as I walked through the doors to fill my voluntary role, George's eyes would light up. "You came!" he would cheer. His enthusiasm was so touching to me that I can picture him saying those words still today. It was with absolute *delight*, the kind that tells you someone has *really* been anticipating your arrival.

Sometimes as I settle in for times of prayer with God, I raise my hands toward heaven and imagine my Father crying out, "You came!"

Romans 15:7 tells us that we aren't merely tolerated by God; we are accepted by Him.

> Therefore, accept each other just as Christ has accepted you so that God will be given glory.

We don't have to be having a good day to enter God's presence. No matter how we're feeling, what we're thinking about, the struggle we're experiencing, or the questions we hold, God's enthusiasm over our arrival is always the same. He says, "You came!"

Pause and Pray

God, it's hard for me to imagine sometimes that anyone gets that excited over my presence, let alone the Creator of the universe. And yet You do! I love knowing that. And I love You. Amen.

Reflect and Write

What expression do you picture on God's face as He says to you, "You came!"?

....

....

....

Care That Keeps Going

> Though you have changed a thousand times,
> He [God] has not changed once.
>
> ———————
>
> CHARLES SPURGEON

Trends come and go. You probably notice this in your own life. What you cared about two years ago is different from what you cared about last year. And what you cared about last year is different still from what you care about now. What we're "into" is always shifting, always being replaced by something else. And yet there is one thing that will never change or shift: God's deep care for you.

This may be hard to believe, but it's true: you are not a passing trend to God. He cares for you every bit as much today as He did a year ago, and that care will remain sure every day of your life. His care for you will never change. His love for you will never dim. His passion for knowing you and relating with you and walking with you will never fade over time.

In Romans 8:38, the apostle Paul writes:

And I am convinced that nothing can ever separate us from God's love. Neither death nor life, neither angels nor demons, neither our fears for today nor our worries about tomorrow—not even the powers of hell can separate us from God's love.

Nothing can keep God's care from coming for you. *Nothing!* He will push through every boundary to find you, to meet you where you are, to wrap His arms around you and let you know that you are safe and loved.

Pause and Pray

God, it's overwhelming to think that You care for me as You do! Thank You for pursuing me so thoroughly, so consistently, so lovingly. It is a gift to be loved by You. Amen.

Reflect and Write

Why do you think God is so committed to caring for His children? Why is He so committed to *you*?

....

....

....

DAY 44

Healing Is Yours

Begin to rejoice in the Lord, and your bones will
flourish like an herb, and your cheeks will glow
with the bloom of health and freshness.

A. B. SIMPSON

In Jesus's day, a leader in the military came to Jesus and begged Him for help, saying, "Lord, my young servant lies in bed, paralyzed and in terrible pain" (Matt. 8:5).

Jesus said He would go and heal the man, but then the military officer paused out of respect for Jesus. "Lord, I am not worthy to have you come into my home. Just say the word from where you are, and my servant will be healed" (v. 8).

The officer knew what it was like to give a command and have people follow it. It's like when your mom or dad uses their "serious" voice or hollers your first *and* middle names. You know you'd better do what they say, or there will be stiff consequences for you. The officer had many soldiers under his command. When he told them to come, they came; when he told them to go, they went; when he told them to do something, they did it—no questions asked.

Jesus was amazed by this man's insight. Turning to the people who were standing by watching this scene unfold, He said, "I tell you the truth, I haven't seen faith like this in all Israel!" (v. 10).

Then Jesus told the officer to go home. "Because you believed," He said to the man, "it has happened" (v. 13).

The young servant was healed that very hour.

Here is what Jesus saw in the officer's life: faith. He believed that Jesus could simply *tell* a sick person to get well and that person's health would be restored. He didn't have to know the person. He didn't have to see the person. He didn't have to touch the person. He simply had to say the word, and it would be accomplished.

Which is how I know this is true: wherever you need power in your life today, whatever kind of healing touch you need, Jesus stands ready to help you out.

I don't know why some people who pray to be healed on this earth are not. Only God knows the answer to that. But what we *are* all promised is the healing touch of God's presence.

If you are frustrated, Jesus can calm you down. If you are lonely, Jesus can enfold you in community. If you are feeling scattered, Jesus can usher in peace. Whatever needs healing in your life right now can be healed with just a word—a word spoken by your Savior, the One who holds all healing in the palm of His hand.

Pause and Pray

God, when I'm sick or angry or heartbroken or afraid, I tend to pursue all sorts of remedies before remembering to turn to You. But none of those remedies ever helps me! You'd think I would quit trying them. Help me to remember that whatever needs healing in my life will find its remedy only in You. I love You, Lord. Amen.

Reflect and Write

What needs healing in your life today? Tell Jesus about it now.

....

....

....

Dream House

> If we discover a desire within us that nothing in this
> world can satisfy, the most probable explanation
> is that we were made for another world.
>
> C. S. LEWIS

I f you could wave a magic wand and have your dream house appear right before your eyes, what would it look like? Would it have fancy pillars in front? Would it be a barn filled to the brim with every possible kind of animal? Would it double as a spaceship that could take you far, far into the unexplored parts of our galaxy?

Inside, would it have a dance studio? A room with a trampoline floor? A library with stacks upon stacks of books? A science lab? Secret tunnels and passageways? Tunnels that run underground? A two-story waterslide? A separate kitchen reserved for baking cupcakes? What would *your* dream house include?

If you're like most people, you dream of a reality that is far different from the reality you're living in. You fantasize about being surrounded by things you love and having all-day access to activities you adore. You envision a wonderful place . . . a better place . . . a place where all is *right*.

In Colossians 3:1–3, the apostle Paul gives some advice to a church that is good advice for you and me today as well. He says this:

Since you have been raised to new life with Christ, set your sights on the realities of heaven, where Christ sits in the place of honor at God's right hand. Think about the things of heaven, not the things of earth. For you died to this life, and your real life is hidden with Christ in God.

Basically, Paul is telling us not to get too hung up on where we live today—in our same old house in our same old neighborhood in the same old zip code we've lived in all our lives—because that address is *going to change*. Those of us who have surrendered our lives to Jesus are destined for a different home . . . an eternal home . . . a heavenly home . . . a dream house to beat all dream houses. In the book of Revelation, we learn that the dream house God is building for us will be the perfect dwelling place, a place where only joy and peace can live. No pain. No sorrow. No frustration. And no chores! How about that for dreamy?

Whatever is frustrating you about life today, remember this: a better place is waiting for you, a place where you'll *truly* feel at home.

Pause and Pray

God, thank You for the promise of a real dream home someday. Help me to stay focused on that coming reality whenever I get discouraged by the one I'm in now. Amen.

Reflect and Write

What do you most look forward to regarding the eternal home you're headed for?

....

....

....

PART 4

So.

Much. Joy.

This may be hard to believe, but it's true: the more we talk
with God, the more we will experience pure joy.

He is waiting for you even now.
How much joy would you like?

Opening the Door

> For years we've been telling God to get out of our schools,
> to get out of our government and to get out of our lives.
> And being the gentleman He is, I believe He has calmly
> backed out. How can we expect God to give us His blessing
> and His protection if we demand He leave us alone?
>
> ANNE GRAHAM

A woman asked me a question recently that I thought was interesting. "Why should we even bother to pray," she said, "if God knows everything anyway?"

I told her that if prayer mattered to Jesus while He experienced earthly life, then it should matter to us. And then I said this: "I believe that God is sovereign over the universe. But I also believe that He likes to be invited into our days, into our situations, and into our lives. Yes, He holds all things together and possesses all power to affect the entire world, if He so chooses. But He much prefers to work *with* us and *through* us rather than bossing us around."

I'm a huge fan of the author C. S. Lewis and have read the entirety of his Chronicles of Narnia series—multiple times. One of my favorite exchanges in the entire series is from the book *The Magician's Nephew*. You may recall that Aslan is the lion who represents God; here is what the characters have to say about him:

"Well, I do think someone might have arranged about our meals," said Digory.

"I'm sure Aslan would have, if you'd asked him," said Fledge.

"Wouldn't he know without being asked?" said Polly.

"I've no doubt he would," said the Horse. "But I've a sort of idea he likes to be asked."*

In Revelation 3:20, the writer John reminds us that God does like to be invited in. Referring to Jesus, he says:

Look! I stand at the door and knock. If you hear my voice and open the door, I will come in, and we will share a meal together as friends.

You may be asking yourself, *If Jesus wanted to come in, couldn't He just bust down the door?* The answer, of course, is yes. But just like Aslan, Jesus likes to be asked. Remember, true love doesn't force its way in. True love is something that's *desired*. We pray, then, not to try to control things in the world that only God can really control. We pray to relate, in love, to God, the One who holds all things in the palm of His hand.

*C. S. Lewis, *The Magician's Nephew*, The Chronicles of Narnia (New York: HarperCollins, 1950), 86–87.

Pause and Pray

God, I sometimes forget that You want to be invited into my life, and yet Revelation 3:20 says plainly that You do. I pray for the courage and the presence of mind to stop throughout my day today and invite You into whatever I'm doing—going to class, working hard at swim practice, hanging out with my friends. I know You're with me always. Today I pray that I will acknowledge Your presence. Amen.

Reflect and Write

How might God feel to be explicitly invited into whatever you're doing?

....

....

....

Delighted

What God delights in about us is that we delight in him.

JOHN PIPER

I have a friend who has thirteen children. I'm serious: *thirteen.* She has no twins, and she adopted zero children. She has been pregnant and delivered a baby *thirteen individual times.* Hard to imagine, right?

One time I asked her how she keeps track of all those kids. She and her family live way out in the country, and I imagined children running all over creation without her knowledge. Do you know what she said? She told me she counts their shoes at the door. If there are only twenty-four shoes by the door, then she knows to go looking for one kid. Brilliant!

While most of my friends don't have *quite* that many children, they do seem to have been born with the "mothering" gene. They played with baby dolls when they were kids. They dreamed of having children one day. They were "naturals" as young mamas . . . always knowing exactly what to do. Me? I wasn't that way. I always loved my friends' kids, even as I never expected to have children of my own. When I became an aunt for the first time, I was excited to hold that darling baby boy. But I was equally excited to hand him back to my sister when he started to wail. If I had thirteen kids, I would *surely* lose a few of them. Which is maybe why God gave me just one.

Back on Day 24, I mentioned a verse that I'd like to circle back to now. Psalm 37:23 says this:

> The LORD directs the steps of the godly.
> He delights in every detail of their lives.

Don't miss this: despite God having many, many more than thirteen children, not only does He keep up with us all, but He also takes joy in every part of our lives. That math test you have next week? He *cares* about that detail. He *takes joy* in knowing about it.

Your upcoming birthday party? He cares about that detail too. He takes joy in knowing about it.

The new girl at school you're trying to befriend, the pimple that just showed up on your cheek, the mom-daughter retreat you just signed up for, the choreography you're working hard to learn in dance class, the fact that you hit a triple in yesterday's softball game, your weird obsession of late with fresh strawberries—God cares about these and ten thousand other details about you, and He takes joy in knowing each one.

Pause and Pray

God, if You really care about the details of my life—and I believe that You do—then I'm going to write down a few details I'd love to share with You about what's been going on with me these last few days . . .

Reflect and Write

What details do you want to share with your loving heavenly Father?
Go ahead and share them now.

....

....

....

Breaking Through

The best way out is always through.

ROBERT FROST

Have you ever worked really hard at something, giving it all you had, struggling with it, failing at it, and then, finally, one day you broke through? All your hard work paid off as you were suddenly able to do that thing you just couldn't do. Maybe it was the splits. (I haven't had that particular breakthrough just yet and am pretty sure I never will.) Maybe it was algebra. Maybe it was learning to enjoy your little brother. Whatever it was, that moment of achievement felt a little bit like flying—a rush of energy taking you higher and higher in the sky.

Here's a secret, free of charge: you can experience breakthrough in prayer too.

You may try and fail at prayer nine hundred and ninety-nine times, frustrated that it seems like your prayers don't get past the ceiling of your bedroom, but on that thousandth occasion, look out! Breakthrough is coming your way.

The truth is that the more you pray, the more you will want to pray. And the better at prayer you'll get.

You'll long to talk with God.

You'll crave His distinctive companionship.

You'll feel restless until you can get time alone with Him.

You'll *relish* those moments with Him.

Spiritually speaking, this is how you know you've reached break-through: you find that you *just must pray.*

When the apostle Paul was giving the Christians in Thessalonica instructions on how to live the Christian life, he told them this:

Always be joyful. Never stop praying. Be thankful in all circum-stances, for this is God's will for you who belong to Christ Jesus. (1 Thess. 5:16–18)

"Never stop praying," Paul told them. Never stop, because when you keep going, keep trying, keep working, keep praying, the day will come when you finally break through.

Pause and Pray

God, I can't wait for this kind of breakthrough! Please help me to persist in prayer until it's mine. Amen.

Reflect and Write

What do you think a breakthrough in prayer will be like for you? How will you feel? How will your habits change? What will be dif-ferent in your relationship with God?

....

....

....

Changed

Few things are more infectious than a godly lifestyle.

CHUCK SWINDOLL

One time I had the privilege of meeting Queen Elizabeth's husband, Prince Philip. I had been invited to Holyrood Palace in Edinburgh, Scotland, to receive an award from him for service to Scotland. It was truly awe-inspiring to see a real, live member of the royal family in person. It's not every day you get to see royalty, and I remember soaking up that experience, never wanting it to end.

Looking back, I see how intentional and special every part of that experience was. For starters, everyone who was there that day—myself included—had dressed very carefully for the occasion. Many of us, I'm sure, had purchased a new dress or a new hat to wear, all because we were going to meet a *royal*. The palace staff had mapped out an entire process for how we would interact with Prince Philip—the order in which we'd stand in the receiving line, where the receiving line would be, what we would be doing before and after meeting him, and so forth. The food and drinks had all been handpicked and were precisely served. On and on it went. Every detail of the afternoon had been carefully laid out.

Now, don't get me wrong. Meeting Prince Philip was an *amazing* thing, a memory I'll not soon forget. And yet at the end of the day, he is still just a person—like you, like me, like us all. All the preparation and planning and fuss got me thinking: How much trouble do we go through to be in the presence of the *living God*?

In 2 Corinthians 5:17, the apostle Paul says:

This means that anyone who belongs to Christ has become a new person. The old life is gone; a new life has begun!

We aren't to put on just new clothes for God; we're to put on a whole new life! We are to allow His transforming work to take hold of our lives so that over time we look more like Him.

Pause and Pray

God, thank You for reminding me that I'm not who I used to be and that I'm changing still today. I give You complete access to my mind and my heart and my habits and my life. Transform me to look more like You! Amen.

Reflect and Write

What is one thing you could do to put on a new life today to look a little bit more like God?

....

....

....

Divine Mirror

Spiritual identity means we are not what we do or what
people say about us. And we are not what we have.
We are the beloved daughters and sons of God.

HENRI NOUWEN

Who do you see when you look in the mirror? How do you define yourself?

student	sister
dancer	writer
soccer player	baker
middle child	cousin
pianist	reader extraordinaire
painter	

You probably fill *many* roles in life, and yet if there is one role God wants you to think about first, whenever you look in a mirror, it's this one: child of the one, true King.

John 1:12 says this:

But to all who believed him and accepted him, he gave the right to become children of God.

It took me many, many years to understand that a child of God was my true identity. My father died when I was just five years old, and for a long time, I thought that was who I was—the girl in class who didn't have a father.

I was wrong. I do have a Father, and so do you. You may have the best dad on the planet, and if that's true, then yay. You may have lost your dad, or you may have a difficult relationship with your dad. Whatever is true for you, I want you to know this: you have a Father in heaven who watches over you, who knows the number of hairs on your head, who calls you "My daughter."

You! Yes, you. You are a child of the King! Whatever you do in life and whoever else you are, never forget this most important fact about you: you are called daughter by the King of Kings.

Pause and Pray

God, there is nothing more precious to me than being regarded as Your child. Thank You for calling me Yours. Amen.

Reflect and Write

What would change about the way you see yourself if you fully embraced your role as God's child?

....

....

....

Perfect Peace

Because of the empty tomb, we have peace. Because
of His resurrection, we can have peace during even
the most troubling of times because we know He
is in control of all that happens in the world.

PAUL CHAPPELL

I didn't meet my husband, Barry, until I was thirty-seven years old, and soon after we were married, for the first time in my life, I found myself longing for a child. Two long years later, I discovered I was pregnant, and my jaw almost hit the floor. *How should I tell Barry?* I wondered. It was one of the most exciting days of my life.

The first few weeks of my pregnancy were a blur of absolute joy. I told total strangers that I was pregnant. I read books to the wee one in my belly. I played an assortment of songs to see whether baby was more into country or pop. At our sonogram, we learned that we were having a boy. It was a happy time in our lives. Until the phone call I received one day.

Because I was an older first-time mom, my doctor had ordered additional tests, and when the results of one of them came back, she sat me down and said that there was something wrong with my baby. *Really* wrong. She said that maybe I wouldn't want to keep the baby, given how wrong things were, but I was determined to have him. "No!" I told her. "I am going to deliver this child. God has a plan for this baby, and I'm holding on to His plan."

For the next few weeks, I was in a pretty dark place. I'd begged God for this baby, and now He was going to take him away from me before we had even met? It felt so unfair.

Barry and I were living by a beach at the time, and one morning I woke up early and drove to the water's edge. Nobody was there . . . just a flock of seagulls and me. I took off my shoes and waded into the shallow water. And I prayed. I prayed like I'd never prayed before, hollering out to God over the wind and the waves and the birds. "Jesus!" I said. "My heart is aching! I don't understand this at all. But I want to declare here and now that You and I are in this thing together. I've always needed You, but right now I *really* need You. I need You more than ever before!"

I told Jesus that I loved Him. I told Him that I would never give up on Him, regardless of what happened with my child. I thanked Him that although He had never promised me an easy life, He had promised that He would never, ever leave me. I renewed my commitment to Him there on the beach. And then I got in my car and drove home.

From that moment on, I quit praying for a perfect pregnancy, a perfect delivery, or a perfect child. Instead, I prayed for the presence of a perfect Father. And guess what? That's exactly what I got. Plus, in the end, my son was born with no problems whatsoever, and he has grown into an amazing man. But I'll tell you this: even if things had turned out differently, God's faithfulness would have shone through. He gave me His perfect presence. He gave me His perfect peace. I call that perfect enough.

In John 14:27, Jesus says this:

I am leaving you with a gift—peace of mind and heart. And the peace I give is a gift the world cannot give. So don't be troubled or afraid.

I don't know what is troubling you today. What I do know is this: if you would like to have perfect peace, you can. God is offering it to you now.

Pause and Pray

God, right here in the middle of all my worries, I will hold on tight to You. I'm not letting go of You for even a moment. Where else would I go to find peace? Amen.

Reflect and Write

What worry can you leave at Jesus's feet today in exchange for His perfect peace?

....

....

....

Real Joy

If you have no joy, there's a leak in
your Christianity somewhere.

BILLY SUNDAY

Have you ever heard the worship chorus that goes, "The jooooy of the Loooooooord is my strength, the jooooy of the Loooooooord is my strength, the jooooy of the Loooooooord is my strength, for the jooooy of the Loooord is my strength"?

It's a fun, old sing-along song, but for those who know Jesus, the lyrics are serious business. We understand that if we are left with what we can do in our own strength, we are going to fail.

Life is hard! People can be difficult! Stress is real! Friends break our hearts! We *need* the strength that God provides us. We need power from on high.

Did you know that one of the ways to access this supernatural strength is to choose joy? Consider the words of Paul in 1 Thessalonians 5:16–18, in which he says:

Always be joyful. Never stop praying. Be thankful in all circumstances, for this is God's will for you who belong to Christ Jesus.

Do you see how intentional these verses are? Paul is not telling us to sit down and wait for joy to hit us but rather to make some strong choices. To choose joy, even when it feels hard. Here are some of the ways to do that: We don't stop praying, even when we feel like quitting. We choose gratitude, remembering all the good things that God has done for us. When we do those things, we find the joy that comes from God alone.

I know life can be tough some days. But never let life steal what's yours in Jesus Christ: joy—the absolute, powerful joy of the Lord, which is your strength.

Pause and Pray

God, thank You for promising to give me joy today. I commit to letting Your joy be my strength. Amen.

Reflect and Write

What might it look like to choose joy today?

....

....

....

The Power of the Word

Don't fall into the trap of reading the
Bible without doing what it says.

FRANCES CHAN

During my senior year of high school, a teacher had me
enter a contest in which I had to recite a speech from
any Shakespeare play. "You have a gift for drama," she
explained, which I'm not sure was high praise. I decided to go for
it anyway.

I first thought about doing something from *Romeo and Juliet*, but
since Juliet was either hopelessly in love or about to die, I decided
to take a pass on her. I picked Katherine instead from a play called
The Taming of the Shrew.

On the day of the competition, I realized I was in over my head.
The other contestants were amazing. I mean, *amazing*. I swallowed
hard, thinking, *I'll never win this thing*.

As it turned out, I was right. But things were even worse than
that.

During my performance, I delivered the lines I'd memorized, but
because I thought they needed to be "jazzed up" a little, I added

some lines that weren't even in *The Taming of the Shrew*. I threw in a couple of Juliet's better lines. I made stuff up. "Whatever it takes!" I figured before finishing, taking a bow, and sweeping off the stage.

After everyone who was competing had taken their turn, the judge took center stage. "Before I announce the winners," he said, "I'd like to invite one of our contestants back to the stage."

Yep. It was me.

When I reached his side, he looked at me and said, "What on earth were you thinking? You can't just *make up* your own lines."

I fumbled around for an explanation, but there was none to be found. He then said something to me I've never forgotten. "The authority is in the text. When you decide to come up with your own lines, you have lost all authority."

Second Timothy 3:16–17 says this:

All Scripture is inspired by God and is useful to teach us what is true and to make us realize what is wrong in our lives. It corrects us when we are wrong and teaches us to do what is right. God uses it to prepare and equip his people to do every good work.

God has given us His holy Word so that we can be taught what is true and change our lives to align with that truth. When we look to other books—other words, other lines—for our source of truth, we lose all authority. The Bible is the believer's ultimate source of authority and truth. By reading its words and applying them to our lives, we will have the spiritual authority to stay faithful to Christ, to stand up for what's right, to be salt and light in our world, and to tell others where hope is truly found.

Pause and Pray

God, I pray I will never add to or take anything away from Your holy Word. Help me to read the Bible every day, to learn what it says, to write its words on my heart, and to live in accordance with its truth. Amen.

Reflect and Write

What one Bible verse can you carry in your heart today as an encouragement to walk in the truth?

....

....

....

Thirsty

The key to Christian living is a thirst and hunger for God.

JOHN PIPER

Have you ever been so thirsty that you thought you might not make it if you didn't find some water fast?

One time when I was on a mission trip in Thailand, I forgot to fill my water bottle. My group had driven high into the mountains, and the temperature was well above 100 degrees. It was h-o-t, hot, and I was *beyond* thirsty. My team needed water too, so it felt selfish to ask for some of theirs. After all, I was the one who had neglected to fill my bottle, not them.

For hours and hours that day, all I could think about was water. I imagined cool drops of that good old H_2O on my tongue, trickling down my throat, hydrating all thirty-seven million of my body's desperate cells. I wanted water. I *needed* water. I had to get some water soon.

In Psalm 42:1–2, the psalmist says this:

> As the deer longs for streams of water,
>   so I long for you, O God.
> I thirst for God, the living God.
>   When can I go and stand before him?

Did you know that once you become a praying girl, you will start to think of prayer like you think of cool water on a hot day? You will think about prayer all the time! You will crave it and long for it and feel spiritually dry without it.

What are you thirsting for today? Recognition? Popularity? Comfort? Satisfaction? Social media likes? That new pair of jeans?

Or is it possible you're longing for the thing that will actually quench your thirst . . . the spiritually hydrating gift known as prayer?

Pause and Pray

God, in the same way that only water can quench my thirst on a super-hot summer's day, I know that only talking with You can quench the thirst I feel inside. Thank You for the gift of prayer, the cool water that hydrates my life. Amen.

Reflect and Write

How do you think God uses girls who crave prayer to solve problems in His great big world? How might He use you?

Fearless Faith

Don't be afraid, for I am with you.
 Don't be discouraged, for I am your God.
I will strengthen you and help you.
 I will hold you up with my victorious right hand.

ISAIAH 41:10

I t had been a routine physical exam, but there was something in my blood work that prompted my doctor to order further tests. When those results came back my doctor detected some suspicious cells and told me I would need to have surgery soon. It was a Thursday afternoon when I received the call, and the procedure was scheduled for Monday.

The following morning I woke early, poured a cup of coffee, headed outside to the porch, and sat down to be with God. As the sun climbed high over the horizon, I walked to the edge of the lake. I got down on my knees. I raised my hands toward heaven and prayed, "Father, this is a surprise to me, but I know it's no surprise to You. Thank You for being with me now and for committing to being with me on Monday. I want whatever will bring You glory, Father. If it will bring You more glory for this to turn out to be cancer— perhaps my hospital bed will be beside someone who doesn't know You yet—then I'm all in. Whatever happens, whatever is Your will, then I say yes. Amen."

The results from the test came back later that day, and the tumor was benign. I didn't have cancer after all.

I tell you this not because I'm trying to say that things will always work out the way you want them to whenever you fall to your knees in prayer. They won't. They don't. You've probably already figured that out. No, I tell you this because I want you to know that stopping in the midst of an upsetting moment to surrender your plans to God will always bring a certain fearlessness to your situation. And once fear is banished, love moves in.

I could have learned that day that I had an awful form of cancer, and in terms of my spiritual experience, the outcome would have been the same. God graciously removed my fear, He restored my faith in His goodness, and He assured me that I'd be okay no matter what the results were. Isn't that all we need in life really—to know that we'll be okay in the end?

The next time something makes you feel afraid, hand that fear over to God. Ask Him to replace it with faith. Trust Him to work everything out.

Pause and Pray

God, I praise You because You are faithful and also because You are good. Thank You for making a way for me to move through life without fearfulness. It's so good to know that I don't have to be afraid. Amen.

Reflect and Write

What are you feeling afraid of today? What would it feel like to lay that fearfulness down?

....

....

....

I Forgive You

Forgiveness is God's command.

MARTIN LUTHER

Have you ever been wronged?

Has a friend told someone a secret you trusted her with?

Have you been called a mean name?

Have you been passed over for a lead role in a recital that you deserved?

Have you been blamed unfairly for something you didn't do?

Here's a question to consider: How did you feel about the person who wronged you?

For most people I know—and I include myself here—the natural reaction when we feel wronged is defensiveness. Or anger. Or disappointment, discouragement, dejection, or sadness. What's *not* so natural? Forgiving the person for what they did.

Here is what Jesus says in Matthew 6:14–15:

> If you forgive those who sin against you, your heavenly Father will forgive you. But if you refuse to forgive others, your Father will not forgive your sins.

That is quite a statement, isn't it? If we refuse to forgive those who hurt us, then God will refuse to forgive us. Yikes! Thankfully, the opposite is also true: if we choose to forgive people when they wrong us, then God will joyfully forgive us. And based on personal experience, I will tell you that if we want to know the power of God in prayer, we simply must forgive. I know it's hard to forgive. I know it feels unfair to forgive. (After all, *they* hurt *us*!) I know it takes great courage to forgive. But forgiveness is worth it every time.

When I think of Jesus suffering a brutal death and choosing to forgive His accusers and abusers *while He was hanging on the cross,* I recognize that I, too, can choose to forgive. I see that it's not *that* hard for me. We can forgive. In fact, we must forgive. To hang on to anger and bitterness is to give Satan an open door into your heart. And you don't want that! It's far better to forgive quickly and completely and to trust God to sort out the rest. Satan has nothing to say to forgiveness. Genuine forgiveness makes him powerless and frustrated and weak. And so, forgive.

No matter what.

Immediately.

Wholeheartedly.

And with great expectation for the freedom to come.

Forgiveness is God's gift to us in a world that's not fair.

Pause and Pray

God, sometimes I think that because of what someone has done to me, I just can't forgive them. It feels like forgiving them will mean telling them that what they did was okay. And what they did to me wasn't okay! It was hurtful and awful and mean. But I understand now that forgiving them doesn't equal excusing what they did. It just means freeing myself from the burden of living with bitterness and rage. I want to be free of those things. I want to live in peace and joy. Forgiveness is the path to get there. Thank You for paving it for me. Amen.

Reflect and Write

Who do you need to extend forgiveness to today? Trust God to give you the strength to do so.

....

....

....

Overwhelming Joy

Laugh 'til you weep.

FREDERICK BUECHNER

Do you have a friend who can always make you laugh? You know the kind of person I mean. Even on the worst day, just seeing that person's face brings a smile to yours. God is a lot like that. He's spilling over with joy, and He's always willing to share.

I've always loved the words of Psalm 30:11–12:

> You have turned my mourning into joyful dancing.
> You have taken away my clothes of mourning and
> clothed me with joy,
> that I might sing praises to you and not be silent.
> O Lord my God, I will give you thanks forever!

When we walk closely with God, keeping lines of communication open between us and Him, it doesn't mean we won't come up against obstacles, struggles, challenges, and very bad days. It just means that those things won't take us down. It means that regardless of everything that's happening around us, we can be clothed not with sorrow but with unwavering, unlimited, overwhelming joy.

Joy is not like happiness. Happiness tends to depend on what's going on around us at the time. If you get good grades, that will make you—and your mom and dad—happy. If you get that puppy you've been asking your parents to get you for a gazillion years, that will definitely make you happy.

But joy goes deeper. Joy is a spiritual gift, part of the fruit of the Spirit. It doesn't depend on your circumstances. It comes from your relationship with your Father in heaven. The more time you spend in God's presence, the more His joy will take over.

Pause and Pray

God, this is a new idea to me that I can laugh in the face of hard times, that I can smile even when struggles are real. Help me to laugh today! Help me to dance with joy today! Help me to sing praises to You and not be silent! Help me to thank You for the good things You have done. Amen.

Reflect and Write

What is one thing you can do today that will bring you joy? What could you do for a friend, your family, or someone who's new at school to share your joy with them?

. . . .

. . . .

. . . .

Standing Strong

There is no neutral ground in the universe;
every square inch, every split second, is claimed
by God and counter-claimed by Satan.

C. S. LEWIS

It was a story that made headlines around the world. A young woman who loved lions was offered a job at a lion sanctuary and decided to move far from home to take the job. She went through extensive training to learn how to care for the lions—how to feed them, how to keep their habitat clean, and, most importantly, how to keep herself safe from these natural predators.

"I don't need safety instructions," she said to herself. "I love lions and have an unusual ability to bond with them. They would never hurt me."

For the first few weeks, the young woman honored the training she'd received, keeping her distance from the lions as she'd been told to do. But one Saturday morning when no other employees were around, she couldn't stand the distance any longer and decided to enter a lion's habitat by herself. She thought she had made a connection with the lion and was eager to approach the lion, to touch the lion, to feel his fur beneath her hands.

And so she did.

And then she paid dearly for her decision.

In a flash, the lion killed that young woman, the same one who thought she'd never get hurt.

It's an awful story, and yet it is a perfect picture of how we tend to regard Satan, another "lion," according to Scripture. Here is what 1 Peter 5:8 says:

> Stay alert! Watch out for your great enemy, the devil. He prowls around like a roaring lion, looking for someone to devour.

Whenever I think of this sad story, I think of the spiritual battle we're in. Satan goes around looking for people to hurt, for people to rip to shreds. He tempts us to sin because he knows that if he can get us to lie to our parents or cheat on a test or betray a friend or steal snacks from a store, then our hearts will harden a little bit toward God. The more we sin, the harder our hearts become, until we are so far away from God that we barely know how to find our way back.

This is why the Bible says to stay alert. To watch out. To remember what we've been told. We simply can't mess around with evil and expect not to get hurt. As we sin, we start to crave sin, and that path leads us to heartache and pain.

But as we pray, we start to crave prayer, and that path leads us to beauty and life. Then we are standing strong!

Pause and Pray

God, please, please keep my feet on the path of righteousness. Help me to stay strong as a praying girl! Amen.

Reflect and Write

What will you do to stay alert today? You might make time to read your Bible. You might set an alarm to help you remember to pray. You might ask a parent to pray for you. You might talk with a friend about checking in with each other to be sure you're prioritizing God's ways.

....

....

....

~~Impossible~~

If we see the possibilities in the
problems, we can have victory.

WARREN WIERSBE

P erhaps you and I will meet someday. I would love that!
I've written books for many years, and each time someone comes up to me and says, "I read your book and
loved it," it makes me very happy. It feels like a gift to me, a gift I
never take for granted.

But until you and I cross paths, may I give you a blessing to carry
with you throughout your days? It is from the very end of the Bible,
from the book right before Revelation. It's such a short book that
if you blink while you're thumbing through the New Testament,
you'll miss it. It's so short, in fact, that it has only one chapter.
Know which book I'm talking about? It's Jude! In Jude 24–25, we
find these words:

> And now to him who can keep you on your feet, standing tall in
> his bright presence, fresh and celebrating—to our one God, our
> only Savior, through Jesus Christ, our Master, be glory, majesty,
> strength, and rule before all time, and now, and to the end of all
> time. Yes. (Message)

Perhaps when you read this passage you think, *Well, that sounds amazing, but how on earth is that possible?* Let me remind you of Jesus's words in Matthew 19:26:

Jesus looked at them intently and said, "Humanly speaking, it is impossible. But with God everything is possible."

That's why we win, my friend. We're not asked to do this life on our own. Jesus has promised to help us every single day, good and bad, easy and hard. There is nothing you will face today or tomorrow that God doesn't care about, and what might seem impossible to you is possible with God.

I am praying for you today. I am praying that you'll stand strong. I am praying that when you fall down you'll run to God, whose arms will be open, waiting for you. I am praying most of all that you will know you are loved, loved, loved.

Pause and Pray

God, thank You for the blessings in my life, and thank You for this blessing today. Amen.

Reflect and Write

Who can you give this same blessing to today? Which of your friends or family members could use this encouragement most?

....

....

....

And the Winner Is . . .

Outside of Christ, I have been defeated;
in Christ, I am already victorious.

WATCHMAN NEE

I t's always fun to watch a competition of some sort on TV when it's the last episode of the season. Whether it's a baking show, a singing show, a dancing show, even a dog show, I always get excited when the host says those four critical words: "And the winner is . . ."

There is always a long pause before the winner is revealed, and during that pause, I can barely breathe. "Well, who is it?" I find myself screaming at the screen. "Just tell us already. Tell us!"

Everyone wants to win, don't they? Nobody enters a competition hoping to lose. And the best news I can share with you is that Christ has already won this battle that you and I are in.

When Jesus triumphed over death and the grave, there was a mighty power shift. Colossians 2:15 puts it this way:

> He stripped all the spiritual tyrants in the universe of their sham authority at the Cross and marched them naked through the streets. (Message)

The New Living Translation says it like this:

He canceled the record of the charges against us and took it away by nailing it to the cross. In this way, he disarmed the spiritual rulers and authorities. He shamed them publicly by his victory over them on the cross. (vv. 14–15)

Because of Jesus, my friend, we win.

I don't know if you feel like you're winning at life today, but if you are a follower of Jesus, then in the ultimate sense, you will always win.

We live in a culture that increasingly dishonors God, that tries to throw God out of schools, that mocks God in movies, but this won't last forever. One of my favorite passages of Scripture is Philippians 2:10–11, which says this:

> At the name of Jesus every knee should bow,
>   in heaven and on earth and under the earth,
> and every tongue declare that Jesus Christ is Lord,
>   to the glory of God the Father.

That's right. Someday *everyone* will bow down before the Lord in humble submission. Someday *everyone* will see that Jesus is King. Someday we will raise our voices to praise our Messiah. And on that day to beat all other days, all of heaven and nature will cry out together, "Believers in Jesus, you *win*! Worthy is the Lamb! Worthy is the Lamb! Worthy, worthy is the Lamb!"

Pause and Pray

God, right now I celebrate that because of Jesus I win. I love You, Lord. Thank You for loving me. Amen.

Reflect and Write

What do you imagine it will feel like when the *entire earth* surrenders to God?

....

....

....

Sheila Walsh is a powerful communicator, Bible teacher, and best-selling author with more than five million books sold. She is the author of *It's Okay Not to Be Okay*, *Praying Women*, and the award-winning *Gigi, God's Little Princess*. She is cohost of *LIFE Today* with James and Betty Robison, with more than one hundred million viewers daily. Walsh is a popular speaker and Bible teacher around the world. She lives in Dallas, Texas, with her husband, Barry, their son, Christian, and their two pups, Tink and Maggie.